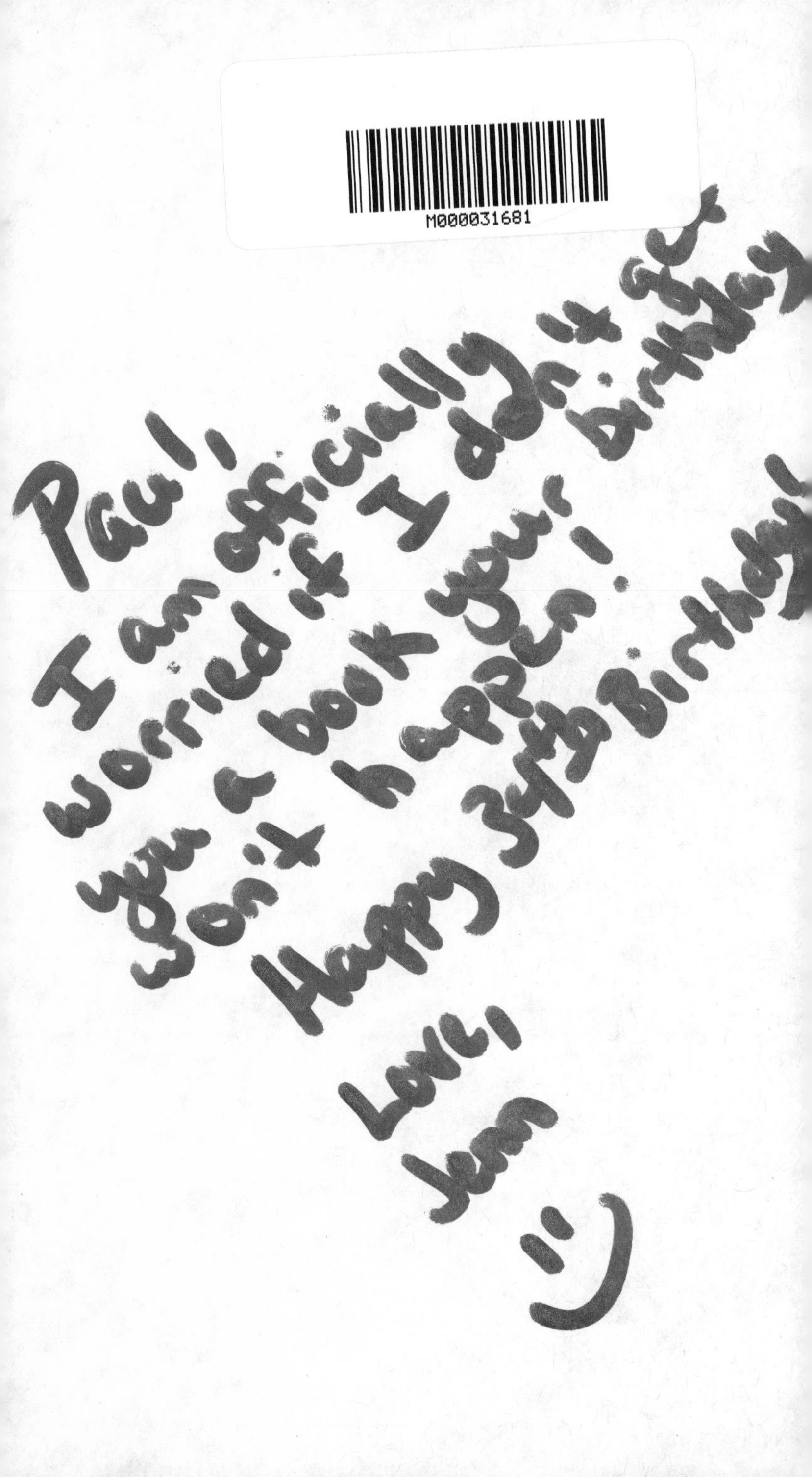

Paul,
I am officially
worried if I don't get
you a book your birthday
won't happen!
Happy 34th Birthday!
Love,
Jenn
:)

The Kingdom of God Is Like . . . Baseball

The Kingdom of God Is Like . . . Baseball

A Metaphor for Jesus's Kingdom Parables

James S. Currie

CASCADE *Books* • Eugene, Oregon

THE KINGDOM OF GOD IS LIKE BASEBALL
A Metaphor for Jesus's Kingdom Parables

Cascade Books
An Imprint of Wipf and Stock Publishers
199 W. 8th Ave., Suite 3
Eugene, OR 97401

www.wipfandstock.com

ISBN 13: 978-1-60899-246-1

Cataloging-in-Publication data:

Currie, James S.

The kingdom of God is like baseball : a metaphor for Jesus's kingdom parables / James S. Currie.

p.; 23 cm.

ISBN 13: 978-1-60899-246-1

1. Jesus Christ—Parables. 2. Baseball—Religious aspects—Christianity. 3. Baseball—History—Miscellanea. I. Title.

BV4501.2 C863 2011

Manufactured in the U.S.A.

To Jo Ann
whose companionship to baseball games
and in life is an indescribable joy

Contents

Acknowledgments

THIS has been a labor of love. It has also been a most challenging project. It could not have been undertaken without the participation of many, often unwitting, kind and faithful friends.

At the outset I thank my parents—my father, who took me to my first minor league baseball game (the Houston Buffs) as well as my first major league game (the Houston Colt .45s), and who would often play catch with me in our front yard on Sunday afternoons, and my mother who signed me up to play Little League baseball where I learned first-hand the sights, sounds, smells, and feel of the game.

I thank my brother, Tom Currie, a much better baseball player than I, and, no doubt, a much more perspicacious theologian than I, but who nevertheless was a constant source of encouragement in this project. He also read several of the chapters and offered some crucial suggestions that improved the text significantly.

Thanks also to my sister, Elizabeth Currie Williams, who also read parts of the manuscript and offered helpful suggestions.

The idea of relating baseball to theology, while not new, first became an opportunity for me to develop through the pastor-theologian program, sponsored by the Center of

Theological Inquiry at Princeton Theological Seminary and directed by the Reverend Dr. Wallace Alston. To him and to that program I am deeply indebted. It provided me with the chance to read, write, and develop *in nuce* some of the ideas presented in this book.

The Reverend Ted Foote, pastor of First Presbyterian Church in Bryan, Texas, and Mrs. Pam Engler, a member of that congregation, invited me to preach and speak there when this effort was in its infancy. Both Rev. Foote and Mrs. Engler are ardent baseball fans, and I will be forever grateful to them for the invitation. It was an experience from which I learned a great deal, but it also led me to dare to think it an idea worth pursuing.

Workshops at Mo-Ranch, a Presbyterian conference center in the Texas Hill Country, and at educational events at the Presbytery of New Covenant also afforded me the opportunity to try out and refine some ideas that appear in this book. I am thankful for their hospitality.

My thanks are also extended to Donald McKim, a baseball aficionado himself, who has written about baseball and theology, who, early on, encouraged me in this project and led me to Wipf and Stock Publishers. I extend my gratitude to Christian Amondson at Wipf and Stock for his willingness to read the proposal and, subsequently, accept it.

Finally, this effort would never have come to fruition without the love, support, and encouragement of my wife, Jo Ann Caldwell Currie, the love of my life. Her reminders to me to keep the reader in mind and to write with passion have been of inestimable value. She herself has become an ardent baseball fan, and it is a joy to watch baseball games, both in person and on television, together.

Introduction

JESUS told stories to describe the kingdom he proclaimed and embodied. The subject matter of those stories was real and familiar in the lives of his hearers—mustard seeds, vineyards, Pharisees and tax collectors. He said that the kingdom of God is *like* . . . , not the kingdom of God *is* . . .

Eugene Peterson maintains that one of the reasons Jesus's use of parables was effective was that they engaged the imagination of the listener. "Parables aren't illustrations that make things easier," Peterson argues. Rather, "they make things harder by requiring the exercise of our imagination, which if we aren't careful becomes the exercise of our faith."[1]

Peterson also suggests that Jesus' use of parables was subversive. He writes:

> Parables sound absolutely ordinary: casual stories about soil and seeds, meals and coins and sheep, bandits and victims, farmers and merchants. And they are wholly secular: of his forty or so parables recorded in the Gospels, only one has its setting in church, and only a couple mention the name God."

1. Eugene Peterson, *Living the Message: Daily Help for Living the God-Centered Life* (New York: HarperOne, 2007), 13–14.

> As people heard Jesus tell these stories, they saw at once that they weren't about God, so there was noting in them threatening their own sovereignty. They relaxed their defenses. They walked away perplexed, wondering what they meant, the stories lodged in their imagination. And then, like a time bomb, they would explode in their unprotected hearts. An abyss opened up at their very feet. He *was* talking about God; they had been invaded![2]

As risky as it may be, it seems appropriate to try to find contemporary language and imagery with which to compare the kingdom, and to do so in a way that illustrates the subversive grace and faithfulness of God with which God surrounds us. Given the inordinate place and the business of sports in American society today, it is even riskier to suggest that there may be characteristics of the kingdom that might be compared to that game. But that is precisely what I propose to do.

There is a difference between making a religion of sport, on the one hand, and seeing facets of a game that resemble features of the life of faith. More than any other sport, baseball, in my view, offers a perspective that resonates with the rhythms of life and can help us better understand the life of discipleship. There is, however, no claim here that baseball is life or, worse, that baseball is the kingdom of God (though there might be some who would dispute that!). Baseball is not a game every aspect of which can or should be examined theologically, any more than Jesus examined every aspect of vineyards theologically.

2. Ibid., 13.

Baseball is a game. Period. But it is a game that offers suggestive parallels with life and, coincidentally and unwittingly, provides spiritual allusions to kingdom life. Joseph Price refers to this spiritual aspect of this sport as the "mythos of baseball."[3]

What is there about baseball, as opposed to other sports like football or basketball or soccer, that lends it to comparisons with the kingdom of God? First, unlike most other sports, baseball has no time clock. That means that there is no artificial time period imposed on the outcome of the game. Second, also unlike most other sports, the game is played every day, or almost every day. In spite of the charge that the game is slow and boring, it is precisely in that respect that the game most resembles the reality of daily life.

Third, except for the dimensions of the infield, every ballpark is different. Distances to the outfield fence may vary from field to field. Some baseball fields are considered a "hitter's ballpark", while the size of other fields may become the favorites of pitchers. Like life, situations are different, and personalities are different. There are not "cookie-cutter" ballparks in baseball, and there are few "one-size-fits-all" answers in life.

Fourth, baseball is both an individual and a team sport. From a batter's point-of-view, it's very much an individual sport. The hitter must respond to whatever the pitcher throws. No one else can do that for him. Whatever he does—swings at a pitch or takes the pitch—it's completely

3. Joseph L. Price, *Rounding the Bases: Baseball and Religion in America*, Sports and Religion (Macon, GA: Mercer University Press, 2006), 77–83, 123–26.

up to him. And yet, it's also a team sport from the batter's point of view. Sometimes a batter is called on to move a runner to second with a sacrifice bunt in order to give the team a better chance of scoring.

Similarly, in the field every player must be prepared to do a job, whether it's catching a fly ball or fielding an infield grounder. At the same time, to turn a double play requires both individual skill and dexterity, but also timing and understanding between players.

Finally, more than any other sport, baseball seems to lend itself to unusual characters. Whether it's Casey Stengel or Yogi Berra, whose mangled grammar made many wonder exactly what each had said; or Pete Gray, who had only one arm and yet played for the 1945 St. Louis Browns; or Eddie Gaedel, a twenty-six-year-old midget who pinch-hit for the St. Louis Browns in the second game of an August 19, 1951, doubleheader against the Detroit Tigers; or Bill Veeck, owner of the St. Louis Browns and later the Chicago White Sox, whose promotional gimmicks became legendary, the game lent itself to the acceptance of peculiar personalities without diminishing the integrity of the game.

I grew up with baseball, playing Little League but never going beyond that. I played catcher and first base most of the time but wasn't all that good. However, in playing the game even at that level, I discovered a kind of magic about the simplicity of the game: a ball, a bat, and a glove were the only equipment needed. The simplicity of the rules of the game itself was part of the magic for me. It was a team sport, and yet it was also a one-on-one matchup between pitcher and batter. Everyone on the field would have a chance at bat.

Then there was the field itself. It was like a stage where players, even at a relatively young age, were expected to perform, whether it was pitching, fielding, batting, or running the bases. All the senses were affected. The aroma of a freshly cut infield grass, accompanied by the sight of freshly laid chalk lines defining the boundaries of the field of play contributed to a sense of an opportunity for a fresh beginning.

When I was growing up in Houston in the late 1950s, my father would occasionally take my brother and me to Buff Stadium, where the Houston Buffs, a minor league team, would play. At the time I didn't know the difference between major league baseball and the minor league game. What I did discover was that here were men playing a game I had played. Same rules and same equipment, but a bigger, more majestic playing field. Apparently, those men were as inexplicably enamored with the game as I was, perhaps even more so.

Branch Rickey, who as general manager or president, laid the foundations for championship teams in St. Louis, Brooklyn, and Pittsburgh, expressed something of the magic of the game when he asserted, "Man may penetrate the outer reaches of the universe, he may solve the very secret to eternity itself, but for me, the ultimate human experience is to witness the perfect execution of the hit-and-run."[4]

In 1962 the Buffs gave way to a major league team, the Houston Colt .45s who were later renamed the Houston Astros. No matter how many times I went to see a game at Colt Stadium or in the Astrodome or now at Minute Maid Park, I was, and am, always awestruck when I walk up from

4. Quoted in ibid., 122–23.

the concourse on the way to my seat, and all of a sudden the whole expanse of a carefully manicured baseball field unfolds before me. It's like a movie in which one's field of vision is limited and then, quite suddenly, everything opens up into a breathtaking vision of beauty.

In an exchange in his novel *Shoeless Joe*, W. P. Kinsella captures something of the magic of a baseball park:

"'Have either of you spent any time in an empty ballpark? There's something both eerie and holy about it.' . . . 'A ballpark at night is more like a church than a church,' I say, as I stop the Datsun on the gravel of the parking lot and turn off the motor and lights."[5]

But if baseball is not life, and if baseball is not religion or theology, what is the relationship between baseball and theology and the Christian life? Just as one can find theological themes in novels, paintings, movies, and other works of art as well as in life "in the world," one can also discover such themes in other, perhaps more playful activities, such as baseball, and that it can be helpful to extrapolate such themes.

Using some of the parables Jesus told, in this book I propose to make connections between some themes in Reformed theology and baseball.

It is my hope that this book will accomplish at least three purposes. The first is to share something of the joy that baseball has given me and many others. The second is to make some of the themes in Reformed theology more accessible to the person in the pew.

5. W. P. Kinsella, *Shoeless Joe: A Novel* (New York: Houghton Mifflin, 1982), 160.

And, most important, the third purpose is to convey the profound and transforming nature of the gospel and the joyful challenge of the life of discipleship.

So, let's play ball!

1

A Game of Failure and Freedom

(Luke 18:9–14)

There are some images that remain imprinted in the memory of baseball fans. Some, such as Bill Mazeroski's ninth-inning home run in the seventh game of the 1960 World Series enabling the Pittsburgh Pirates to defeat the heavily favored New York Yankees, reflect the thrill of victory (at least for the Pirates and their fans). Others depict the agony of defeat, such as the groundball that went through Boston Red Sox first baseman Bill Buckner's legs in Game Six of the 1986 World Series with the New York Mets, an error that, in all likelihood, cost the Red Sox not only the game but the World Series itself.

It is often noted that a hitter is considered successful if he gets a hit in three out of ten attempts. Considered one of the best hitters in the history of the game, Ted Williams was the last player to hit over .400 in a single season (he hit .406 in 1941), and his career batting average was .344. Interrupted twice by military service, first in World War

II and then in the Korean War, Williams's career includes some rather remarkable statistics.

When he retired in 1960, he ranked only behind Babe Ruth and Jimmie Foxx in home runs, seventh in runs batted in, and seventh in career batting average (but first among players in the post-1920 "live-ball" era). Nevertheless, with his 2,654 hits Williams still made 5,052 outs, 709 of which were strikeouts.

In his twenty-two-year career Babe Ruth's batting average was .342. He had 2,873 hits in 8,399 at-bats. Although he had 714 home runs, he also struck out 1,330 times.

Brad Lidge, "closer" for the Houston Astros and then the Philadelphia Phillies, is, unfortunately, best remembered by some for the three-run home run he surrendered to Albert Pujols in Game Five of the 2005 National League Championship Series between Houston and St. Louis. While Houston eventually went on to win that series and participated in its first-ever World Series, that home run seemed to affect Lidge, psychologically, for the rest of his career in Houston. Lidge experienced greater success with the Philadelphia Phillies in 2008 when he saved forty-four games without a blown save and led his team in winning the World Series against the Tampa Bay Rays.

A more tragic case is that of Donnie Moore. In a career that spanned thirteen seasons, Moore pitched for five different teams (the Chicago Cubs, St. Louis Cardinals, Milwaukee Brewers, Atlanta Braves, and California Angels). Although he posted a respectable record (43 wins and 40 losses, 89 saves, and a career 3.67 earned-run average), Moore is most remembered for one pitch he made in Game Five of the 1986 American League Championship

Series when the California Angels were facing the Boston Red Sox.

The Angels had a three-games-to-one lead in the series and were leading 5–4 in this particular game. If they won this game, they would go to the World Series for the first time ever in their history. With two outs in the ninth inning and a runner on first base, Moore was called in from the bullpen to get the final out. He gave up a home run to Dave Henderson, which put the Red Sox ahead 6–5. The Angels scored one run in the bottom of the ninth, sending the game into extra innings. Moore stayed in the game and eventually gave up a run in the eleventh on a sacrifice fly to Henderson. The Red Sox won the game, 7–6, and went on to win the series in seven games.

Three years later, after bouts with severe depression, alcoholism, and drug abuse, Moore, whose performance in 1986 was often blamed for the Angels' failure to make it to the World Series, shot his wife, Tonya, and then shot and killed himself. His wife survived the shooting.

Or consider Fred Snodgrass, centerfielder for the 1912 New York Giants. In the eighth and final game of the World Series (one game actually ended in a tie) Snodgrass dropped a routine fly ball in the tenth inning, enabling the Boston Red Sox to win the game, 3–2, and the Series, four games to three with one tie. Jim Reisler writes that that muffed fly ball "haunted Snodgrass the rest of his days: 'Hardly a day in my life, hardly an hour, that in some manner or the other the dropping of that fly doesn't come up,' he told an interviewer in 1940." Reisler goes on to note that even in the headline of Snodgrass's obituary that one incident could not be forgotten: "'Fred Snodgrass, 86, Dead, Ball Player Muffed 1912 Fly.'"[1]

Or earlier still is the case of Fred Merkle. In a game at the Polo Grounds against the Chicago Cubs on September 23, 1908, rookie first baseman Merkle unwittingly committed a blunder that cost the New York Giants a win. With two outs in the bottom of the eleventh inning and the game tied 1–1, Merkle was on first base with a single, and teammate Moose McCormick was on third base. Giants batter Al Bridwell ripped a single to right field, apparently scoring McCormick with the winning run.

Merkle ran about sixty feet towards second base. Seeing that McCormick would score the winning run, he peeled off the base path and headed towards the clubhouse, avoiding the crowd that had begun to swarm the field; everyone assumed the Giants had won the game. The Cubs remained on the field, and second baseman Johnny Evers demanded to have the ball. Having retrieved a ball (no one is sure if it was the actual game ball), he stood on second base and screamed for the umpire to call Merkle out on a force play, thus nullifying McCormick's (winning) run. Home plate umpire Hank O'Day, having anticipated this, since a similar play had occurred a few weeks earlier in which no force out was called (as was the custom on a hit that went beyond the infield), called Merkle out.

In spite of the fact that Merkle had done what all players had done up to that point and nothing had ever been called, in spite of the fact that Merkle went on to play in six World Series over a career that spanned nineteen years

1. Jim Reisler, *The Best Game Ever: Pirates vs. Yankees, October 13, 1960* (New York: Carroll & Graf, 2007), xvii.

(1907–1926) and four teams (the Giants, Dodgers, Cubs, and Yankees), in spite of the fact that Merkle was considered one of the most intelligent and decent players in the game, he was ridiculed, demonized, and scapegoated for years afterwards. Even in retirement he and his family experienced embarrassing taunts of being a "bonehead."

In the late 1940s Merkle's reputation underwent a rehabilitation. Primarily through the efforts of Brooklyn Dodgers broadcaster Red Barber, the media began to appreciate the career of Fred Merkle as well as the grace with which he had handled misguided and unfair criticism. Merkle died in Daytona Beach, Florida, on March 2, 1956 at the age of sixty-seven.[2]

It seems that there are far more instances of failure than success, some more serious than others. The Chicago Cubs are often reminded that the team hasn't been to the World Series since 1945 and hasn't won the Series since 1908. And yet in the history of the World Series the Cubs have at least gone to the Series ten times (in 1906, 1907, 1908, 1910, 1918, 1929, 1932, 1935, 1938, and 1945). Many franchises would consider that a storied history. And indeed it is, except for the fact that the Cubs have not been back to "the fall classic" in over sixty years.

The Boston Red Sox were similarly caricatured until they made it to the Series in 2004 when they swept the St. Louis Cardinals in four straight games. As if to prove that "the curse of the Bambino" had been truly erased, they

2. A full account of Merkle's career as well as of the 1908 "incident" can be found in Mike Cameron's book, *Public Bonehead, Private Hero: The Real Legacy of Baseball's Fred Merkle* (Crystal Lake, IL: Sporting Chance, 2010), 91–94.

accomplished the feat again in 2007 by taking four straight from the Colorado Rockies.

No matter how successful a player or a team may be, baseball is about failure. Or as Christopher Evans and William Herzog put it, "baseball in American culture, both individually and socially, is often about losing—a fact that cannot be overturned by faith in a just God."[3]

Political columnist and ardent baseball fan George Will begins the Introduction to his book *Men at Work: The Craft of Baseball* with the following story:

> A few years ago, in the Speaker's Dining Room in the U. S. Capitol, a balding, hawk-nosed Oklahoma cattleman rose from the luncheon table and addressed his host, Tip O'Neill. The man who rose was Warren Spahn, the winningest left-hander in the history of baseball. Spahn was one of a group of former All-Stars who were in Washington to play in an old-timers' game. Spahn said: "Mr. Speaker, baseball is a game of failure. Even the best batters fail about 65 percent of the time. The two Hall of Fame pitchers here today [Spahn: 363 wins, 245 losses; Bob Gibson: 251 wins, 174 losses] lost more games than a team plays in a full season. I just hope you fellows in Congress have more success than baseball players have."[4]

3. Christopher H. Evans and William R. Herzog II, *The Faith of Fifty Million: Baseball, Religion, and American Culture* (Louisville: Westminster John Knox, 2002), 218.

4. George F. Will, *Men at Work: The Craft of Baseball* (New York: Macmillan, 1990), 1.

Jesus tells a story of two men who went up to the temple to pray. Both were losers, but only one of them knew it. In fact, one thought he was so good that even God should be impressed. The other thought so little of himself that he is driven to his knees and can hardly bear to address God.

"'Two men went up to the temple to pray, one a Pharisee and the other a tax collector. The Pharisee, standing by himself, was praying thus, "God, I thank you that I am not like other people: thieves, rogues, adulterers, or even like this tax collector. I fast twice a week; I give a tenth of all my income." But the tax collector, standing far off, would not even look up to heaven, but was beating his breast, and saying, "God, be merciful to me, a sinner!"'"

Both men are sinners because both men are human, but the one (the tax collector) understands and admits his own sinfulness, while the other (the Pharisee), by proudly pointing to his own apparent goodness, exhibits the truth of the doctrine of human depravity. Luke concludes this story by citing Jesus's own response to the scene: "'I tell you, this man [the tax collector] went down to his house justified rather than the other; for everyone who exalts himself will be humbled, and he who humbles himself will be exalted" (Luke 18:9–14, NRSV).

One point of the parable is that all human beings are sinners, and the sooner we recognize and acknowledge that, the sooner we will be able to hear and rejoice in the good news that in Jesus Christ God shows his love for us, forgives us, and beckons us into his service, always doing the best that we can, not with the thought that somehow we can please or appease God or endear ourselves to God in spite of our foolishness, but simply because this loving, gracious, and forgiving God has created us and claimed us as God's own, and loves us to the end (John 13:1b).

One of John Calvin's wonderful contributions to theology was the third use of the law. The first two uses of the law are negative, designed to condemn or restrain. The first use is theological; that is, the law condemns human beings for their disobedience and unrighteousness before God. The second use of the law is political; that is, it serves to restrain human beings "who are untouched by any care for what is just and right unless compelled by hearing the dire threats in the law."[5]

Calvin adds a third use, the moral use, which is positive. This use sees the law as a gift. Indeed, Calvin sees this use as "its principal use, which pertains more closely to the proper purpose of the law" and "finds its place among believers in whose hearts the Spirit of God already lives and reigns."[6] Unlike the first two uses of the law, which serve as correctives to human sinfulness, the third use of the law views the law as a gift, a guide, as "the goal toward which throughout life we are to strive."[7]

Whereas the Pharisee takes pride in how righteous he has been and makes a point of letting God know how good he's been, the tax collector falls to his knees acknowledging his own sinful nature and his own inability ever to be righteous before God. And yet, paradoxically, it is in that very acknowledgment that the tax collector discovers his

5. Calvin, *Institutes of the Christian Religion*, ed. John T. McNeill; trans. Ford Lewis Battles et al., 2 vols. (Philadelphia: Westminster, 1960), II.vii.6,10.

6. Ibid., II.vii.12.

7. Ibid., II.vii.13.

true freedom. There is no longer any need to try to prove himself to God or anyone else. He may start each day with the brutally yet refreshingly honest confession, "God, be merciful to me, a sinner." And in that bedrock confession he hears God's word of grace and acceptance that enables him to live that day with the freedom to live, knowing that he cannot be perfect, knowing that he does not have to earn God's approval, but also knowing that out of gratitude he is free to do the very best that he can, whatever that might look like.

It is in the paradox of acknowledging who we are as imperfect, sinful human beings, not only that we hear God's word of grace, but that we are also able to live life with a new sense of freedom and joy. This paradox is beautifully expressed in George Matheson's hymn "Make Me a Captive, Lord":

> Make me a captive, Lord,
> And then I shall be free;
> Force me to render up my sword,
> And I shall conqueror be.
>
> I sink in life's alarms
> When by myself I stand;
> Imprison me within Thine arms,
> And strong shall be my hand.
>
> My heart is weak and poor
> Until it master find;
> It has no spring of action sure.
> It varies with the wind.
>
> It cannot freely move

Till Thou has wrought its chain;
Enslave it with Thy matchless love,
And deathless it shall reign.

My will is not my own
Till Thou hast made it Thine;
If it would reach a monarch's throne,
It must its crown resign;
It only stands unbent
Amid the clashing strife,
When on Thy bosom it has leant,
And found in Thee its life.[8]

Knowing that even our very best will fall far short of perfection does not mean that either we should not try or that we make excuses for our failure. It's who we are, and when we acknowledge that, we are free to give our very best, regardless of the endeavor because we never know when that little bit of extra effort can make the difference in a project. We might surprise ourselves.

So it is in baseball. No one is perfect. Don Larson, who is the only person, so far, to pitch a perfect game in a World Series (Game 5 in 1956), finished his career with a record of 81 wins and 91 losses—at best a fairly mediocre record. Even if a hitter goes four-for-four one day, he still must start over the next day, just like the hitter who went oh-for-four.

Evans and Herzog are right, at least in part: baseball is about losing. Sometimes talent wins out over hustle and hard work. Occasionally, as in the case of the 1960 Pittsburgh Pirates, hustle and hard work win out. Evans

8. Hymn no. 378 in *The Presbyterian Hymnal* (Louisville: Westminster John Knox, 1990).

and Herzog remind us that "in baseball, as in life, faith that our good works (and our suffering) somehow will offer the promise of a better future guarantees us nothing but disappointment. Perhaps the only theological moral we can draw from the examples of the Brooklyn Dodgers and the Boston Red Sox is that 'God allows rain to fall upon the just and the unjust' (but it rains harder on teams with less talent), and nothing we do, or try to do, can stop that."[9]

I recall a parishioner who wondered why there was a prayer of confession in the worship service every week. Before I could offer a reply, he observed that he supposed it was probably there because, while he didn't feel the need to confess his shortcomings every week, there would always be someone who did, even if it wasn't the same person each week.

While there is no requirement that a prayer of confession be part of a worship service each week, its presence reminds us who we are as human beings, namely, that we are flawed, limited creatures and fall far short of the glory of God. But if there is a prayer of confession, there *must* be an assurance of pardon, and that reminds us that we belong to a God who is "merciful and gracious, slow to anger and abounding in steadfast love" (Ps 103:8).

Indeed, because we in the Reformed tradition believe in prevenient grace (literally, grace that "comes before"), we confess our sinful nature in the assurance that we have already been forgiven. Therefore, we live in the joy and the freedom that we belong to a God whose forgiveness does not depend on our confession, but rather who has already

9. Evans and Herzog, *The Faith of Fifty Million*, 218.

forgiven us before we are even aware of our shortcomings, let alone before we have confessed them.

Because baseball is an everyday sport, every day is an opportunity to live in the freedom of new possibilities. Whether one roots for the Cubs or the Astros, the Royals or the Mariners (to name teams that rarely, if ever, make it to the World Series), if one understands one's own flaws and imperfections, then each season, each series, each game becomes an opportunity to do one's best—not to demonstrate or prove that one is better than anyone else, but simply to do the very best one can do, and to do it graciously.

Try as they might to avoid making a bad call, even umpires are not immune from blown calls or public humiliation after clearly blown calls in critical situations. On June 2, 2010, the Detroit Tigers hosted the Cleveland Indians. Armando Galarraga was on the mound for the Tigers. Through eight innings he had faced the minimum number of batters. He had a perfect game.

After getting the first two batters out in the top of the ninth inning, Galarraga faced the Indians' Jason Donald. Donald hit a ground ball to the right side of the infield. Tiger first baseman Miguel Cabrera fielded the ball and threw to Galarraga, who was racing to first base to make the force out. Clearly, Galarraga tagged the base with the ball in his glove before Donald reached the base. Game over. Perfect game. Except for the fact that first base umpire Jim Joyce called Donald safe. In disbelief Galarrage looked at Joyce and, to the surprise of everyone, simply smiles. He went back to the mound and got the last out.

There was no question that the replay showed that Donald was out. Galarraga had indeed pitched a perfect game. But the blown call by the umpire denied him that honor. The remarkable thing about the entire episode was the aftermath. Upon seeing the replay after the game, Joyce admitted his error and apologized. His embarrassment was reflected in his comments: "'It was the biggest call of my career, and I kicked the (stuff) out of it,' Joyce said, looking and sounding distraught as he paced the umpires' locker room after the Tigers' 3-0 win. 'I just cost that kid a perfect game. I thought (the runner) beat the throw. I was convinced he beat the throw, until I saw the replay.'"[10]

The next day Joyce was the home plate umpire. Customarily, before each game the umpires meet at home plate to exchange the lineups with the managers or coaches from each team. Tiger manager Jim Leyland sent Armando Galarraga out to do the honors. In full view of everyone Galarraga and Joyce shook hands. So touched was Joyce by this gracious gesture that he had to wipe away tears.

One reporter wrote: "This one, too, could have ended in rancor but for the sportsmanship shown by both men. Galarraga, who smiled in apparent disbelief after the call, returned to the mound and recorded the last out to end the game. Joyce, an umpire since 1989, apologized, as he did again Thursday, for missing the call.

"'They (Galarraga and Tigers manager Jim Leyland) were as sportsmanlike and as gentlemanly as could be,' Joyce said Thursday during a pregame conversation with reporters during which he paused to wipe away tears. 'I cannot believe the outpouring of support I've gotten, not

10. Associated Press, "Ump Flaws Tiger's Rare Gem," *Houston Chronicle*, June 3, 2010. Online: http://www.chron.com/disp/story.mpl/sports/bb/7033787.html/.

only from my fellow umpires but all my friends, my family and, frankly, you guys.

"'I can't thank you enough. I can't thank the people enough. I'm a big boy. I can handle this. It's probably the hardest thing I've ever had to go through in my professional career, without a doubt.'

"'I'm the same,' Galarraga said Thursday before the game. 'I thought he (made) a mistake, and nobody's perfect.'"

Later in the article the reporter observed: "Away from the ballpark, the grace and good sportsmanship reflected by Galarraga and Joyce had some wondering why they can't see such behavior more frequently in sports, politics and every other walk of life."[11]

Many have read or heard the classic poem, "Casey at the Bat" which was penned by Ernest Lawrence Thayer in 1888 and first appeared in the *San Francisco Examiner*. It is the story of how "the Mudville nine" come up to bat in the bottom of the ninth inning trailing their opponents, 4–2. The first two batters ground out. The next two batters get base hits, leaving it up to "mighty Casey", the one on whom everyone pins their hopes, to win the game. The last stanza of the poem tells the story of the outcome:

> Oh, somewhere in this favored land the sun is shining bright;
>
> The band is playing somewhere, and somewhere hearts are light.

11. David Barron, "Bad Ending, but Great Sports," *Houston Chronicle*, June 4, 2010.

> And somewhere men are laughing, and some-
> where children shout;
>
> But there is no joy in Mudville—mighty Casey
> has struck out.[12]

Thayer's poem ends with Casey's failure to get on base, let alone win the game with a home run. From that point of view, it reflects the dashed hopes of baseball fans everywhere, for who hasn't hoped against hope that when their team is behind and comes up for its last at-bat, there won't be a rally to win the game? What's more exciting than a walk-off home run? But it didn't happen with the Mudville nine.

At least it didn't happen in Thayer's poem. Twenty-two years later, however, Grantland Rice, one of the prominent sports journalists in the first half of the twentieth century, wrote a poem bearing the title "Casey's Revenge." In it the time is a week later. During the week everyone "from the mayor down the line" expresses disappointment with Casey. Even Casey himself "began to sulk and loaf—his batting eye went lame." But another chance comes his way against the very pitcher who had struck out Casey the week before. The bottom of the ninth inning arrives with Mudville behind, 4–1. The first three batters get on base (one hit, one hit batsman, and one walk). The next batter fouls out to the catcher, and his successor flies out to the right fielder. Whose turn is it but Casey's?

> A dismal groan in chorus came—a scowl was on
> each face—

12. Ernest Lawrence Thayer, "Casey at the Bat," in *Classic Baseball Stories*, ed. Jeff Silverman (Guilford, CT: Lyons, 2003), 21.

When Casey walked up, bat in hand, and slowly
took his place;
His bloodshot eyes in fury gleamed—his teeth
were clinched in hate,
He gave his cap a vicious hook and pounded on
the plate.

Even at this point the crowd is hissing and booing, offering no support or hope. The first two pitches are called strikes, but Casey makes no complaint to the umpire.

No roasting for the umpire now—his was an easy
lot;
But here the pitcher whirls again—was that a rifle
shot?
A whack—a crack—and out through space the
leather pellet flew—
A blow against the distant sky—a specie against
the blue.

Above the fence in center field in rapid, whirling
flight
The sphere sailed on—the blot grew dim and
then was lost to sight,
Ten thousand hats were thrown in air—ten thousand threw a fit—
But no one ever found the ball that mighty Casey
hit.

Rice's closing stanza contrasts sharply with Thayer's:

Oh, somewhere in this favored land dark clouds
may hide the sun,
And somewhere bands no longer play and children have no fun,

> And somewhere over blighted lives there hangs
> a heavy pall;
> But Mudville hearts are happy now—for Casey
> hit the ball.[13]

Casey failed the first time, and, no doubt, many times—just as we all do. But Grantland Rice knew that, generally, baseball does not afford players only one chance. Usually, there is another opportunity. In life every day is another opportunity, not necessarily to succeed, but to live as one of God's free and forgiven people.

There is great freedom that comes with knowing we don't have to be perfect. Doing the best we can is hard enough. And doing the best we can, even if it means "failure," can be doubly difficult. But we do it trusting the veracity of the words that we hear every Sunday and need to hear every day, "In Jesus Christ we are forgiven. Thanks be to God!"

13. Grantland Rice, "Casey's Revenge," in *Classic Baseball Stories*, ed. Jeff Silverman (Guilford, CT: Lyons, 2003), 23–28.

2

A Game of Hope

(Luke 15:3–7)

Every year since 1986 in Chicago there has been a Cubs Convention. Primarily an attempt to publicize the Cubs and generate interest in the upcoming season, this gathering takes place on a weekend in January. The last time the Cubs went to the World Series was 1945. The last time the Cubs won a World Series was 1906. The Cubs own the dubious distinction of having the longest title drought in North American professional sports.

The Cubs have become a romantic favorite for many fans because of the combination of their talent and their long inability to reach the fall classic. This portrait becomes even more sympathetic because each year Cubs fans—like most fans everywhere—begin the season with the hope that this could be the year they go all the way. In an article in the *New York Times*, Dave Seminara quotes baseball writer Roger Kahn: "You may glory in a team triumphant, but you fall in love with a team in defeat."

Seminara closes his article by quoting sixty-nine-year old Cubs fan Ronnie Wickers, who has been to most of the Cubs home games over the past forty years: "Being a Cubs fan is just like medicine, it keeps me alive. Players come, players go, but they can't fire me, they can't trade me. I'm always a Cubs fan."[1]

Never giving up is a characteristic that is not unique to baseball. In all sports, indeed in all endeavors, at least in this life we are encouraged never to give up, no matter how hopeless the situation may seem. We may be tempted to throw in the towel, regardless of the particular circumstances, but somehow we muster the gumption to persevere, perhaps not even knowing why we do.

It may be a difficult time in a marriage. It may be a less than stimulating job. It may be a time when work cannot be found. But we persevere with the hope that the situation will not only change but improve. Sometimes, it seems, we persevere because we feel like we have no other choice. And perhaps that, too, reflects a kind of hope because we don't—or can't—give up or give in.

The same is true in baseball, especially in baseball, as, more than any other sport, it resembles life in that it is played day-in and day-out. Because the season is so long, and because games are played almost every day, a team in third, fourth, or fifth place in May could very well compete for the division title if they get on a roll while other teams experience a slump.

Much is made, and rightfully so, of the dramatic game-winning home run by Bobby Thomson in 1951 when

1. Dave Seminara, "Still Stung by Failure, Cubs Fans Convene to Refresh Faith," *New York Times*, January 18, 2010.

the season ended with the New York Giants tied with the Brooklyn Dodgers. Thomson (of the Giants) hit his home run in the bottom of the ninth inning off of Dodgers' pitcher Ralph Branca. What many may not recall is that on August 9 the Giants were fifteen games behind the Dodgers, and many believed the Dodgers had the pennant sewn up. The Dodgers had dominated the series between the two teams that summer. They had even taunted the Giants after a series sweep in early August. Led by the strong pitching of Branca, Carl Erskine, Preacher Roe, Don Newcombe, and midseason addition Clem Labine, and by the fielding and batting of Pee Wee Reese and Jackie Robinson, the Dodgers seemed destined to be in first place from the beginning to the end of the season.

But in the middle of August things began to change. From August 12 to 27 the Giants won sixteen games in a row. In that time span they cut the Dodger lead to five games. The Dodgers pitching staff began to tire. Angered by the taunting of the Dodgers, the Giants players began to play inspired baseball. They were led by Thomson and outfielders and future Hall of Famers Willie Mays and Monte Irvin and by pitchers Sal Maglie, Dave Koslo, and Larry Jansen. And while it's true that Leo Durocher, manager of the Giants (and former manager of the Dodgers) instituted a means of stealing signs from the Polo Grounds clubhouse in centerfield, the effectiveness of that ploy is questioned because many of the Giants players found it distracting and refused to comply with Durocher's scheme.

By the last day of the regular season the Giants had tied the Dodgers. A three-game playoff series would be played beginning October 1 to decide the winner of the

National League pennant and the opponent of the Yankees in the World Series. The Dodgers won the coin toss to determine which team would host Game 1 and which team would host Game 2 and, if necessary, Game 3. Strangely, Charlie Dressen, manager of the Dodgers, chose to host the first game at Ebbets Field, reasoning that if the Dodgers won the first game, they would only have to win one of two games at the Polo Grounds.

The Giants won the first game, 3–1, with Bobby Thomson hitting a two-run home run off Ralph Branca, who threw 133 pitches that day. The Dodgers won the second game, 10–0, at the Polo Grounds. In Game 3 the Giants' Sal Maglie took the mound against Don Newcombe of the Dodgers. The Dodgers took a 1–0 lead in the top of the first inning when Jackie Robinson singled home Pee Wee Reese. The Giants tied it in the bottom of the seventh inning on a sacrifice fly by Bobby Thomson scoring Monte Irvin. In the top of the eighth Brooklyn scored three runs to take the lead, 4–1. That lead held up going into the bottom of the ninth inning.

Newcombe had pitched a complete game the previous Saturday and then five-and two-thirds innings in relief the next day, the final day of the regular season. And now, he had pitched into the ninth inning of this third playoff game.

Alvin Dark singled. Don Mueller followed with another single through the right side of the infield, moving Dark to third. Monte Irvin popped up for the first out. Whitey Lockman then laced a double to left field, scoring Dark, making the score 4–2. Mueller moved to third base, but twisted his ankle in his slide and, in doing so, tore some tendons. He was carried off the field on a stretcher and was replaced by Clint Hartung.

At this point Dodger manager Charlie Dressen took Newcombe out of the game. Would Dressen call on Carl Erskine or Ralph Branca? Or even Preacher Roe, who not only was well rested, but also had limited Bobby Thomson to a .220 batting average over his career. But Roe was not even warming up.

Although his arm must have been tired, according to Clyde Sukeforth, the Dodgers' bullpen coach, Branca "was showing off" in the bullpen because he wanted to pitch the next day against the Yankees.[2] Dressen chose Branca over the more rested Erskine.

Thomson had hit a two-run home run off Branca in Game One of the playoff series, and he had hit several home runs off him over the course of the season. Thomson already had two hits in this game.

Branca's first pitch to Thomson was a fastball for a called strike. His second pitch was up and in. Thomson swung and hit it down the left field line, clearing the fence at the 315 foot marker, sending the Giants to the World Series the next day against the Yankees. Had Thomson not hit the game-winning home run, rookie Willie Mays was on deck. Although Mays had a strong rookie season and would become a Hall of Famer, he had only gotten one hit in ten at-bats in the playoffs and was batting only .222 since September 1. In retrospect, some have wondered why Dressen did not have Branca walk Thomson and pitch to

2. Joshua Prager, *The Echoing Green: The Untold Story of Bobby Thomson, Ralph Branca and the Shot Heard Round the World* (New York: Vintage, 2008), 207.

Mays.[3] Lots of questions have been laid at the feet of Charlie Dressen in that playoff series, but then hindsight is always twenty-twenty.

This dramatic game was immortalized by Giants broadcaster Russ Hodges shouting into the microphone with both the incredulity and the joy most Giants fans must have shared: "The Giants win the pennant! The Giants win the pennant! The Giants win the pennant!"

The Giants lost the World Series to the Yankees in six games. It was the first World Series for two rookies and future Hall of Famers, Willie Mays for the Giants and Mickey Mantle for the Yankees.

There have been other dramatic collapses (or comebacks, depending on one's perspective). In 1964 the Philadelphia Phillies had a six-and-a-half game lead with twelve games left to play in the regular season. Jim Bunning had pitched a perfect game on Father's Day that year, and manager Gene Mauch was expected not only to win Manager of the Year but to take his team to the World Series. The Phillies then proceeded to lose ten games in a row while the Cincinnati Reds won nine in a row. The Phillies and the Reds finished tied for second, one game behind the St. Louis Cardinals, who went on to beat the Yankees in the World Series in seven games.[4]

The 1969 season was the eighth for the New York Mets. They had never finished higher than ninth place in a ten team league. In 1962, their first season, they lost 120 games, a record that still stands. Through forty-one games in 1969

3. Ibid., 213.

4. For an account of the 1964 World Series see David Halberstam's *October 1964* (New York: Villard, 1994).

they had won eighteen games and lost twenty-three. Then they won eleven games in a row.

The Mets were in second place for most of the season, behind the Chicago Cubs. But in mid-August they had slipped to third place, nine and a half games behind the Cubs. But the Mets went on a tear, winning thirty-nine of their final fifty games, and finishing in first place, eight games ahead of the Cubs. The Mets went on to sweep the Atlanta Braves in the National League Championship Series, three games to none, and to defeat the Baltimore Orioles in the World Series in five games.

"It ain't over till it's over," in words that are attributed to Yogi Berra.

In Luke 15 Jesus tells three parables in a row. The first two are very brief. The third is much longer and will be considered in the next chapter. In the first parable, Jesus tells of a shepherd entrusted with a hundred sheep. He discovers that one is lost, so he leaves the ninety-nine to go search for the one that has wandered off. After finding it, he returns to the others rejoicing that he has found the lost sheep.

In the second parable, Jesus tells of a woman who has ten silver coins. She loses one, and then turns her house upside down looking for it. Finally, she does find it and calls her friends together to share her joy in finding something valuable that had been lost.

At the end of each of those parables Jesus says virtually the same thing, namely, "there will be more joy in heaven over one sinner who repents than over ninety-nine righteous persons who need no repentance" (Luke 15:7); and "there is joy in the presence of the angels of God over one sinner who repents" (Luke 15:10).

Neither the lost sheep nor the lost coin does anything of which they can repent. The sheep can wander off and get lost, but it's not a human being that can say "I'm sorry," or "Forgive me." And the coin is simply an inanimate object. It's simply there, unable to will itself to be lost or found. It's the woman who has misplaced it. She's the one who is responsible for it, just as it's the shepherd who is responsible for overseeing the hundred sheep in his care.

At least one of the points of these two parables lies in the persistence of the shepherd and the woman in searching for what is lost. The shepherd leaves the rest of the flock to go look for this sheep that may not even know it's lost, or it may have fallen off a cliff hanging perilously to a tree root growing out of the side of the mountain with vultures circling above and waiting for the sheep to fall to its death. The woman overturns furniture, takes everything out of her closet, and cleans out all the cabinets in search of her lost coin.

Nothing is too much for either until they find what was lost. They pursue their goal relentlessly—filled with hope and expectation. They don't know if they will find what's lost, but giving up is not an option.

While Jesus talks of repentance in both parables, the parables he tells reflect the kind of dogged, relentless, persistent desire to reclaim what was lost. It's a desire that expects to find what was lost.

The fact that the shepherd has ninety-nine other sheep doesn't diminish the importance or value of the one sheep that was lost. The fact that the woman had nine other silver coins doesn't mean that the one that was lost is any less valuable to her. Therefore, both rejoice when they find their lost sheep and coin.

Living with hardheaded, persistent hope—no matter how bleak the outlook may be—is what is called for. It means playing the game with the same kind of expectancy, enthusiasm, and energy when one is a benchwarmer as when one is in the starting lineup, when one's team is in last place as when one's team is in first place.

The Old Testament prophet Hosea captures this passionate longing of God for a people, even when they have strayed from God's ways:

> When Israel was a child, I loved him,
>   and out of Egypt I called my son.
> The more I called them,
>   the more they went from me;
> they kept sacrificing to the Baals,
>   and offering incense to idols.
> Yet it was I who taught Ephraim to walk,
>   I took them up in my arms;
>   but they did not know that I healed them.
> I led them cords of human kindness,
>   with bands of love.
> I was to them like those who lift infants to their cheeks.
>   I bent down to them and fed them . . .
> How can I give you up, Ephraim?
>   How can I hand you over, O Israel?
> How can I make you like Admah?
>   How can I treat you like Zeboiim?
> My heart recoils within me;
>   my compassion grows warm and tender.
> I will not execute my fierce anger;
>   I will not again destroy Ephraim;

for I am God and no mortal,
    the Holy One in your midst,
    and I will not come in wrath. (Hosea 11:1–4, 8–9)

Here the passion and compassion of God is clearly seen in a way that surprises many when they think of the God of the Old Testament as a stern or angry God. In fact, however, the patient, persistent God of Hosea is the same God Jesus describes in the two parables recorded in Luke 15.

Francis Thompson develops this notion of determined and persistent hope on the part of the searcher in his poem, "The Hound of Heaven." Rather than the sheep and the coin, however, Thompson describes a person seeking to escape God.

I fled Him, down the nights and down the days;
I fled Him, down the arches of the years;
I fled Him, down the labyrinthine ways
Of my own mind; and in the mist of tears
I hid from Him, and under running laughter.
Up vistaed hopes I sped;
And shot, precipitated,
Adown Titanic glooms of chasmed fears,
From those strong Feet that followed, followed after.
But with unhurrying chase,
And unperturbed pace,
Deliberate speed, majestic instancy,
They beat—and a Voice beat
More instant than the Feet—
'All things betray thee, who betrayest Me.'[5]

5. Francis Thompson, "The Hound of Heaven," in *The Hound of Heaven and Other Poems* (Boston: International Pocket Library Corporation, 1936), 11.

The writer of Psalm 139 also writes of the inescapability from God:

> O LORD, you have searched me and know me.
> You know when I sit down and when I rise up;
> you discern my thoughts from far away.
> You search out my path and my lying down,
> and are acquainted with all my ways.
> Even before a word is on my tongue,
> O LORD, you know it completely.
> You hem me in, behind and before,
> and lay your hand upon me.
> Such knowledge is too wonderful for me;
> it is so high that I cannot attain it.

Then the psalmist goes on:

> Where can I go from your spirit?
> Or where can I flee from your presence?
> If I ascend to heaven, you are there;
> if I make my bed in Sheol, you are there.
> If I take the wings of the morning
> and settle at the farthest limits of the sea,
> even there your hand shall lead me,
> and your right hand shall hold me fast.[6]

It's that kind of expectant hopefulness that God demonstrates towards us. God never gives up on us, even when we are blissfully unaware that we are lost or foolish or too discouraged to go on. God's hardheaded and persistent pursuit of us lies at the base of the never-give-up attitude we are called to exhibit. In God's service we are called to offer the very best that we have in whatever we do—whether

6. Psalm 139:1–10.

it's in relationships or in a particular project or in play. The point is not that we win, but that we strive for excellence, giving every ounce of energy we can muster.

And it's that same attitude that, at their best, baseball players exhibit. Chris Coste was a member of the Philadelphia Phillies when they won the World Series in 2008. He was later involved in a trade that sent him to the Houston Astros, where he played in 2009. What many may not know is that Coste was thirty-three years old when he finally was called up to the major leagues in 2006. Who knows how long he will be able to stay? But after he had been playing baseball since age seven, and after he spent eleven years in the minor leagues, his determination and doggedness were rewarded.

There are many who were just as determined and dogged who did not make it to the major leagues. A very small percentage of major league aspirants ever actually reach that goal. And yet, often it is in the trying, in playing the game as hard as one can, in fully expecting to succeed that we exceed even what we think possible. That hope, that hardheaded persistence and expectancy, leads to a newfound joy.

3

A Game of Joy

(LUKE 15:11–32)

Ernie Banks was the first African American to play for the Chicago Cubs. He played his entire major league career for that organization (1953–71). In spite of his own impressive personal statistics (for example, 512 career home runs, National League Most Valuable Player in 1958 and 1959), Banks never played in a World Series. This shortstop, who later played first base for the Cubs, exuded a joy for the game that was contagious.

According to Joe Posnanski, Banks, who first signed with the Kansas City Monarchs (part of the Negro Leagues) in 1950 when he was nineteen years old, learned to play the game from Buck O'Neil, a first baseman and later manager of the Monarchs. "Buck said no, Ernie Banks knew how to play, but what he did learn was how to play the game with love. Banks began each baseball game by running up the dugout stairs, taking them two at a time. He then breathed in the humidity, scraped his cleats in the dirt, and shouted what would become his mantra: "It's a beautiful day for a ballgame. Let's play two."[1] (O'Neil served as a scout for the Chicago Cubs, becoming responsible for acquiring both Banks and Lou Brock. In 1962 the Chicago Cubs signed O'Neil as a coach, making him the first black coach in the major leagues.)

Many professional baseball players are so good that they make it look easy. Of course, it's fun if you are doing what you want to do, and if, in addition, you are good at it. Who wouldn't want to go outside everyday and play a kid's game and, by the way, be paid well for it?

Of course, what often goes unnoticed is the amount of work that's involved in reaching the skill level professionals have reached. Technology has led to much more preparation by each player for each game. No longer is it simply a matter of stretching, running, taking batting practice, and warming up before each game. Hitters watch videotape of opposing pitchers to try to pick up tendencies that might be helpful; they also watch videotape of themselves, especially if they are in a slump, to try to correct any bad habits they might have developed. Pitchers do the same by trying to pick up weaknesses in hitters they will oppose. And if they have had bad outings recently, examining videotape may reveal some of their own tendencies that need to be corrected. Preparation has become a year-round endeavor. Some players play winter ball in Latin America. Others have their own rigorous workout regimen in the off-season.

1. Joe Posnanski, *The Soul of Baseball: A Road Trip through Buck O'Neil's America* (New York: Morrow, 2007), 3.

While some may take some time off, very few major leaguers take the kind of time off that was the case fifty or sixty years ago.

And yet, with all the preparation that's required to play the game well today, baseball remains a game, and a game of joy at that. To see Ozzie Smith race onto the field and do a couple of somersaults before taking his place at shortstop; or to see Hunter Pence run into the dugout at the end of an inning with a huge smile on his face; or to hear Ty Wigginton, a veteran of several seasons and several teams, say that seeing the Major League Baseball emblem on his uniform is "cool": to see or hear all this is to be reminded that while it is a game that requires a tremendous amount of work, baseball is still fun. And part of the fun, the joy, of the game is found precisely in the demanding nature of the game.

Towards the end of his biography of Yogi Berra, Allen Barra reflects on one of the characteristics of a Yankee clubhouse with Yogi there:

> People always talk about a guy being "good in the clubhouse" but they never say exactly what that means. When I was in the Yankee clubhouse before important games, I could tell one primary difference between the Yankees and their opponents. It wasn't professionalism—the Yankees were professional, of course, but all ballplayers were professional. What was different about the Yankees is that in all situations, even when they were down, they were always eager to get out on that field and play. And it seemed to me that a lot of that started with Yogi. He always reflected that truth that says you play a game much better

> if you enjoy it. Outside the ball park, he was business, but on the field, in the clubhouse, you could always sense that more than just business, you could feel his joy at being a ballplayer.[2]

The parable of the Prodigal Son is the third in a trilogy that Jesus tells in Luke 15. The theme of all three—the Lost Sheep, the Lost Coin, and the Prodigal Son—has to do with the joy of finding something that was lost. It is Jesus' story about the prodigal that draws our attention in the context of the joy of the gospel.

The story certainly does not start on a pleasant note. The younger of two sons goes to his father requesting his portion of the inheritance that, upon his father's death, will go to him. The father obliges, and the younger son leaves to experience his new-found freedom. We hear nothing of what the father might have said, if indeed he said anything. And we certainly, at least at this point, hear nothing from the older son. And, what of his mother? She doesn't show up anywhere in the account.

So far, the story is all about the younger son. He leaves family, home, security, and apparently discovers independence, new lands, and pleasurable entertainment. But when his money runs out, he begins to discover some of the advantages he had (unwittingly) enjoyed at home. Not only that, but, more important, he also realizes his own foolishness.

It's not simply that in his immaturity the younger son desires immediate gratification in every way. But in addition, as Robert Farrar Capon points out, by demanding his

2. Allen Barra, *Yogi Berra: Eternal Yankee* (New York: Norton, 2009), 363–64.

portion of the inheritance, the younger son is as much as saying that he wishes his father were dead.[3]

So far, there's not much joy. Even in receiving what he has requested—or demanded—of his father does not bring the younger son true joy. The father gives him what his son asks for, knowing that it will not bring fulfillment to his son, and yet also knowing that only his son can learn this hard lesson.

Only after he has gone through his inheritance does the younger son begin to realize that maybe he has made a mistake. It's not that now he has nothing of what he started out with (as though if he still had the money he would be happy and fulfilled). Rather, it's that in "coming to himself" he realizes what he had at home was more than the creature comforts he was missing feeding the pigs. It was the relationship with ones who loved him and whom he loved. He had disrespected and abused that love.

And so, he comes to himself and begins the journey home. It is a journey that, in his mind, required repentance. Such repentance demonstrates to his family and, more important, to himself that he has recognized his own foolishness, disrespect, and disobedience. We've all been there, and the younger son grows in our admiration and respect because we understand the humility and the courage to do what he planned to do.

3. Robert Farrar Capon, *The Parables of Grace* (Grand Rapids: Eerdmans, 1988), 137. Capon's exact words are as follows: "In other words, he tells his father to put his will into effect, to drop legally dead right on the spot. Obligingly enough, the father does just that: he gives the younger son his portion in cash, and to the elder brother, presumably, he gives the farm."

But, miracle of miracles, surprise of all surprises, what happens? As he approaches his father's farm and is going over the speech he plans to give his father, he cannot believe his eyes. He sees his father running to greet and welcome him home. Much is made of the way in which, by this act, the father breaks all rules of decorum. Running out to welcome home a son who was disobedient, selfish, and irresponsible would be uncomely of a father.

And yet, as Capon observes, the father sees a dead son who has come alive: "The father simply sees this corpse of a son coming down the road and, because raising dead sons to life and throwing fabulous parties for them is his favorite way of spending an afternoon, he proceeds straight to hugs, kisses, and resurrection."[4]

The joy of the father and the joy of the son are incomparable. Having experienced death, the son experiences resurrection—not by his own doing but through the unconditional and irresistible grace of his father. It signifies a new life, a new beginning. "The past is finished and gone, behold, the new has come," Paul writes (2 Corinthians 5:17). The past is not forgotten, but we can let go of it. It need not dominate our thoughts or actions. We are invited, even commanded, to be present to the present, having grown wiser and more gracious from our experience of grace.

The joy of the resurrection is not some kind of superficial, disingenuous, plastic happiness that is transparent even to the casual observer. Rather, it is something that profoundly touches one's innermost being. It is something so desirable, so valuable, of such importance that one will do anything for it—even die for it. Perhaps there is something

4. Ibid., 139.

of that meaning in the passage in Hebrews that describes Jesus as "the pioneer and perfecter of our faith, who for the sake of the joy that was set before him endured the cross, disregarding its shame, and has taken his seat at the right hand of the throne of God" (12:2).

Eugene Peterson observes, "The truth is, there aren't very many happy people in the Bible. But there are people who are experiencing joy, peace, and the meaning of Christ's suffering in their lives." He goes on: "Joy is the capacity to hear the name and to recognize that God is here. There's a kind of exhilaration because God is doing something and, even in a little way, it's enough at the moment."[5]

In the summer of 1981 several members of my family and I were hiking in the Rocky Mountain National Park in Colorado. After all of us had reached one destination, one of my sisters, Liz, and I decided to continue onward and upward towards a peak beyond the point we had already reached. We set out, without a trail, and began to realize that under any circumstances this was not going to be an easy task. As the afternoon wore on, dark clouds began to roll in. Knowing that it was neither desirable nor wise to be above the timberline in a thunderstorm, we aborted our ascent and immediately began heading towards the nearest line of trees.

In doing so, however, we headed *away* from the trail that had brought us to our original destination. While there was no lightening, we were sprinkled with rain. Eventually, we gratefully reached the timberline, but there was still no

5. Interview at the beginning of Peterson's book *The Contemplative Pastor: Returning to the Art of Spiritual Direction* (Grand Rapids: Eerdmans, 1993), 5–6.

trail. Now we found ourselves comfortably out of danger of lightening strikes, but having little clue as to which direction to take. We knew we wanted to head downward, and we knew we wanted to stay near the roaring creek that we had accompanied on our way down, but where that would take us was unclear.

In the meantime, the darkness of the trees overhead was soon followed by the darkness of the skies above them. We began to realize that it would be wiser to stop for the night than to try to continue moving in the darkness. We found a rock overhang and huddled beneath it. Only then did it occur to me that, in all likelihood, there was wildlife in these forested mountains. We then realized that between us we had one box of raisins.

The night was long, dark, cold, and sleepless.

The peeking of light that came with the dawn was accompanied by the relief that we had made it through the night. Although tired from little more than an occasional dozing off in the night, we found a new kind of energy that now at least we knew which way was east and had the sun to guide us.

We crept out of the rock overhang that had sheltered us for the night, made our way across the creek that had been our companion on the way down the day before, and began chasing the light of the sun. We found ourselves crossing moraines—climbing one tree-covered hill, descending the other side, and then finding another one to climb again. In the distant skies we saw helicopters which, we imagined, were National Park rangers, notified by our families of our absence, in search of us.

Finally, as we reached the top of one more moraine we saw and recognized one of the well-known peaks in the park. At last, something familiar! Our pace quickened. More moraines. More helicopter sightings, but because of the trees they could not see us waving to them.

And then there was another sighting. A beautiful, sandy, human-made trail! We were close to something or someone that would lead us back. To our right we saw a hitching post for horses, so we took the trail to the left. We were ecstatic, overjoyed. As many trails as we had followed to lakes, up mountains, and all over the national park, never before had we been so happy to see this one!

When we passed persons on the trail heading in the direction of the hitching post, we knew we were close to civilization and could soon contact our family members. Eventually, we reached a dude ranch of sorts, were able to contact family and national park officials, and relax a bit.

The joy that Liz and I had experienced after a night of fear and uncertainty is difficult to express. At different points over the previous eighteen hours of lostness each of us had, alternately, experienced moments of discouragement, and at those times one had offered encouragement to the other. Then came the moment of joy! It was indeed joy at knowing there was no longer need to be afraid and that that time of being lost was over with. But, simultaneously, it was also joy at a renewed appreciation for paths that others had built that would lead us to where we needed to be. It was a renewed gratitude for family. It would not be too much to say that there was a renewed respect and love for life.

Maybe it was something like that the prodigal experienced.

The joy is not so much in the relief that a season of pain and suffering is over with, so much as it is in discovering and receiving God's gift of full love for and acceptance of us as God's own and, furthermore, God's call to us to exhibit that character of kingdom life in, to, and for others. To quote Paul again, "it is no longer I who live, but Christ who lives in me" (Galatians 2:20).

Part of the joy of baseball is the challenge of the game. The challenge includes the preparation, the failures, the training, the demand of the game for our very best. That is true of other endeavors for which one might have a passion.

Kingdom life is like that. It is difficult, if not impossible. And yet, that is what we are called to do, namely, having experienced the joy of God's love, forgiveness, and grace, we are free to try to live the impossible. Who can do what Christ calls us to do in the Sermon on the Mount? No one but Jesus himself. And yet, he calls us, not only not to hate our enemies, but to love them; not only not to retaliate when someone attacks us, but to embrace that person; not only not to worry about what we should eat, drink, or wear, but to trust that God will provide.[6]

In David James Duncan's novel *The Brothers K* there's a point at which the narrator, who happens to be a member of the family described in the novel, reflects on the various views of Jesus held by other members of his family: "It's strange the way everybody has their own pet notion about Jesus, and nobody's pet notion seems to agree with anybody else's. Grandma, for instance, says He's "just a defunct social reformer." Then there's Papa, who once said He's God's Son all right, and that He survived the crucifixion just fine, but

6. Matthew 5:43ff.; 5:38ff.; and 6:25–34.

that the two-thousand-year-old funeral service His cock-eyed followers call Christianity probably made Him sorry He did."[7]

What a shame it is that the joy of the gospel has been lost for many, and that the entire enterprise of Christianity has become little more than a long funeral service.

The joy of baseball is in the game itself, just as the joy of the kingdom is in the kingdom itself. In wanting to give our very best, we know that we will not get a hit every time or pitch a shutout every game. Indeed, some may never get a hit or ever pitch a shutout. It doesn't matter. Having said that, giving our very best shot is part of the joy also. And what if we fail? No matter. If we sulk at our feeble efforts, no matter how good or how poor, we resemble the older son who would not allow himself the possibility of joy in the kingdom.

The joy of the kingdom is experienced in its finding us rather than anything we do. So it is in baseball. How good we are at the game is secondary to the joy of playing the game itself.

7. David James Duncan, *The Brothers K* (New York: Doubleday, 1992), 60.

4

A Game of Community

(MATTHEW 13:33)

ALTHOUGH there are exceptions, usually those who are in the starting lineup play only one position. Mickey Mantle (New York Yankees) played centerfield, Willie McCovey (San Francisco Giants) played first base, Eddie Matthews (Milwaukee Braves) was a third baseman, Derek Jeter (New York Yankees) normally plays only shortstop, Ryan Howard (Philadelphia Phillies) usually plays only first base.

Baseball has always been a team sport, but in recent years it has become even more so. There has been a rise in specialties: pinch hitters, utility players, long-relief pitchers, short-relief pitchers, closers, and, in the American League, designated hitters. Depending on whether a pitcher throws right handed or left handed, the manager may choose to use left-handed pinch hitter or a right-handed pinch hitter.

But even beyond these specialties, a team usually develops a sense of community. Some of that comes simply by playing and being around each other every day. Some of it comes by going through winning streaks and losing streaks together. Some of it comes with the antics of jokers. Some of it is simply the chemistry of the various personalities on the team.

However the community is formed, everyone on the team is part of it. Some contribute more on a regular basis, some contribute less, but all are part of it. The player who sits on the bench most of the time may be called on to pinch hit in a crucial situation. That same player also may contribute by understanding and accepting his limited role as well as by encouraging others.

Baseball is not unusual in this respect. The same can be found in an orchestra, for example, or a band or a choir. Indeed, any group or organization, if it is to function effectively and harmoniously, needs to have members who know their roles, but needs also to appreciate the smallest role.

In one of the shortest of his parables, Jesus compares the kingdom of heaven to "yeast that a woman took and mixed in with three measures of flour until all of it was leavened" (Matthew 13:33). One of the fascinating features of this parable is the use of the yeast image. For instance, yeast almost imperceptibly contributes to the flavor and texture of the bread as it is being baked. Indeed, the yeast itself eventually dissolves or dies in fulfilling its ultimate purpose of creating a healthy loaf of bread. The same can be said of salt, a metaphor Jesus uses to describe kingdom people in the Sermon on the Mount (Matthew 5:13).

This image of yeast contributing to a well-baked loaf of bread without, in the end, leaving any visible evidence of its presence offers a lesson for the church. In the kingdom, as Jesus describes, the focus of attention is on the kingdom, not on the kingdom's participants. No matter how great or how small the role, all are invited to participate in, contribute to, something God has already begun. Indeed, sometimes those who are least conspicuous may make a contribution far beyond what anyone else thought possible.

In writing to the troubled church at Corinth, the Apostle Paul employed the image of the human body to describe how the church, at its best, functions. If we understand the church both as the proclaimer of God's kingdom as well as the provisional representative of that kingdom, then the analogy of the body can be used to describe the kingdom.

Paul characterizes the healthy body as one in which the various parts function in a healthy, coordinated way. What the arm does, it does well. The foot cannot do what the arm does, but it does do what the foot is supposed to do. The eyes see, the ears hear, the nose smells, the fingers touch, the tongue tastes. The parts are not interchangeable, and the body is considered healthy when each part performs its purpose. The eye cannot be a toe, the stomach cannot be the liver, and the lung cannot be the heart.

But they all need each other. Furthermore, when one part of the body hurts, the whole body is affected and is in pain. The heart, lungs, feet, hands, arms, and legs may be fine, but if a person has a toothache, the whole body is in pain.

Similarly, if all parts of an orchestra are playing their parts well, but the timpani comes in at the wrong time or the viola is out of tune, then the whole performance is affected. The same is true for a choral performance. If the bass section misses its entrance, then the whole choir is thrown off. If one person is a prima donna, thinking that he or she should be heard above all others, then that will diminish the beauty of the performance.

In the late nineteenth and early twentieth centuries many who espoused the theology of the Social Gospel, stressing the church's responsibility to bring about the kingdom of God in the world, were also baseball fans. It was not unusual for Washington Gladden (1836–1918) and Shailer Mathews (1863–1941) to employ the notion of teamwork above self as an image of the individual Christian's responsibility to society on behalf of the kingdom of God.

In her book *A Consuming Faith: The Social Gospel and Modern American Culture*, Susan Curtis writes:

> Gladden struck upon the perfect metaphor for explaining the common interests of the individual and the group—the baseball team. Like other social gospelers, Gladden urged Protestants to think of work and salvation as a baseball game. A boy alone may be trained "for any given position on the field," he argued, "but if he undertook to study it out alone it would not be easy for him to understand it. The team work is the whole of it." So it was with life—to strive alone stripped life and work of their "whole meaning

> and significance." "The team work," he repeated, "is all there is of it."[1]

The team is greater than the sum of the individuals on the team. Each contributes to the whole like yeast does to bread.

In David James Duncan's novel *The Brothers K*, the main character is Hugh Chance, a washed-up baseball player, married and the father of six children, and a worker at a paper mill in the Pacific Northwest. He has lost the use of a thumb in a factory accident. However, after the thumb is surgically replaced with one of his big toes, Chance gradually regains the use of his pitching hand with his thumb/toe.

Even though his serious professional playing days are over, at one point Chance is able to hook up as a player and pitching coach with a minor league team in Portland, Oregon. A southpaw, he is at least ten to fifteen years older than most of his teammates. But he is also the best pitcher on the team. When he is on the mound, everyone else relaxes and plays better.

Throughout the book the narrator is one of Chance's sons, Kinkaid. He describes the effect his father's presence on the mound has on the rest of the players:

> With Papa on the mound, the young Tugs for some reason seemed to get a whole new lease on their ballplaying lives. Instead of a potentially glorious, in point of fact underpaid, nerve-wracking, tenuous career, baseball began to seem like a decent way to simply pass a summer's evening. *Look at that sinkerball!* they'd say. *Look*

1. Susan Curtis, *A Consuming Faith: The Social Gospel and Modern American Culture* (Columbia: University of Missouri Press, 2001), 46–47.

> *at that fastball for chrissake. You can be old and busted down as the Toe-man and still play this damned game. And look at him grin back at his bullpen. Look how much fun the old fart's having! That's the way you do it!*
>
> Watching Papa have his fun, many of the young players began to have trouble recalling just where their anxieties and personal crises had been located. Their body language would change. They'd begin to make wisecracks and dumb cracks and old-fashioned novocaine-brained baseball chatter. Then, as far as [manager] Hultz or anyone else could tell, they'd stop thinking entirely and just play ball for the pleasure of it—and it is a well-known fact that when entire teams stop thinking and start playing for fun, wonderful things happen.[2]

Hugh Chance's ageless enthusiasm for the game, even at his relatively old age (for a baseball player) was infectious, enabling his younger teammates to (re-)discover the joy and the fun that the game was intended to provide.

But the community of baseball goes beyond the players on the team. There are, of course, the manager and the coaches. There are the umpires, without whom the game loses much of its order and structure.

In professional baseball there are the announcers, who bring the sights and sounds of the game to those who cannot be at the game. Some of those contribute almost as much to the game's atmosphere as the players and coaches. Anyone who heard Pee Wee Reese and Dizzy Dean announce CBS's

2. David James Duncan, *The Brothers K* (New York: Doubleday, 1992), 287.

"Game of the Week" can remember learning much about the game as well as hearing many funny stories of the game.

The fact that announcers are inducted into the Hall of Fame is an indication of the importance they bring to the game. Some of the best-known radio and television baseball broadcasters have included Red Barber, Jack Brickhouse, Harry Caray, Mel Allen, Jack Buck, Vin Sculley, Ernie Harwell, Harry Kalas, Gene Elston, Jon Miller, Bob Uecker, Milo Hamilton, and Bob Costas. All contribute or have contributed humor, character, and color to the game as well as, of course, descriptions of the play-by-play of the game.[3]

Some of these announcers have been in the profession so long that they have become as much celebrities as many of the ballplayers have, and, among other things, have written their own books.[4]

In addition to those radio and television announcers, baseball writers have contributed mightily to the game—both those who cover the game on a daily basis as well as those who have written books about the game.[5] Baseball

3. For stories by some of these announcers, see Curt Smith, ed., *The Storytellers: From Mel Allen to Bob Costas: Sixty Years of Baseball Tales from the Broadcast Booth* (New York: Macmillan USA, 1995).

4. For example, Red Barber's *Rhubarb in the Catbird Seat* (Garden City, NY: Doubleday, 1968); and *Jack Buck: "That's a Winner"!* (n.p.: Sports Publications, 1999). Both these books, like most of the others, are ghostwritten.

5. The list of outstanding columnists and authors on the subject of baseball could go on and on, but some of the better-known ones include Red Smith, Mickey Herskowitz, Roger Kahn, Roger Angell, Thomas Boswell, David Halberstam, Robert Creamer, George Vecsey, Frank Deford, Leigh Monteville, Tom Verducci, and Peter Golenbeck.

has been the subject of several works of fiction[6] as well as monographs having to do with particular seasons, individuals, or even specific World Series. Beyond that, movies have been made that focus on baseball.[7]

All these are to baseball as yeast is to bread. They contribute to the richness and texture of the game. They point to the nuances, quirks, and characters of the game. Similarly, God's kingdom is made up of quirky and humorous characters as well as those who are pretty straight arrows.

Still another feature of baseball that contributes to the game, and without which it would be diminished, and that is the crowd, the spectators, the fans.

While it may be true that the game will be played whether there are forty thousand or forty persons in the stands, few would argue that the atmosphere is far different in those two circumstances. It's the same game that's played between the first-place team and the last-place team in April that's also played between two teams in the World Series.

6. David James Duncan's *The Brothers K* (New York: Doubleday, 1992) has already been mentioned. Among some of the others are Ring Lardner, *You Know Me Al: A Busher's Letters* (New York: Scribner, 1925); Douglass Wallop's *The Year the Yankees Lost the Pennant* (New York: Norton, 1964); W. P. Kinsella's *Shoeless Joe* (Boston: Houghton Mifflin, 1982), and *The Iowa Baseball Confederacy* (Boston: Houghton Mifflin, 1986); and Mark Harris's *Bang the Drum Slowly, by Henry W. Wiggen* (New York: Knopf, 1956).

7. Among others, such a list would include *The Pride of the Yankees* (the story of Lou Gehrig); *The Stratton Story*; *Bull Durham*; *Field of Dreams* (based on Kinsella's novel *Shoeless Joe*); *A League of Their Own* (a story of women playing baseball during World War II, based on a true account); *For the Love of the Game*; and *The Rookie* (based on a true story).

And yet it's not the same game. For one thing, there's much more at stake in October than there is in April. For another, there's an intangible electricity in the air when the stands are full. The excitement is almost palpable. The fans can make a difference. Photographs taken of games in the late nineteenth and early twentieth centuries show spectators sitting on the field of play (usually in the outfield) and in foul territory, making even more obvious the participatory role the fans played in the game itself.

Of course, some fans can become too involved. In 2003 the Chicago Cubs played in the National League Championship Series against the Florida Marlins. The Cubs had won three of the first five games in the best-of-seven-game series. Game Six was played at Wrigley Field in Chicago. In the top of the eighth inning with one out and the Cubs leading 3–0, Florida Marlin Juan Pierre had reached second base with a double. Mark Prior pitched to Luis Castillo of the Marlins.

Castillo hit a long foul ball towards the left field wall. As Cubs left fielder Moisés Alou reached up to grab the ball, a fan, Steve Bartman, reached out to catch the ball. While the Cubs argued for fan interference, the umpires ruled that the ball had left the field of play and allowed Castillo to continue his at-bat.

The Marlins went on to score eight runs in that inning and won the game, 8–3, tying the series at three games apiece. If fan interference had been called, Castillo would have been out, and Prior and the Cubs would have needed to retire one more batter to finish the eighth inning. The Marlins went on to win Game Seven and the right to play the American League champions, the New York Yankees. The Marlins won that World Series four games to two.

The Cubs were five outs away from winning the right to play in their first World Series since 1945, and a fan played a major role in preventing that from taking place.

More often than not, however, participation by the fans, whether they are pleased or not, is understood to be an integral and fair part of the game. And there is the extended baseball audience listening to the radio or watching on television. All are part of the game, and all, whether immediately at the game or vicariously at home or in a car, participate in the game. Just as players, coaches, broadcasters, and fans have different roles in a baseball game, so every follower of Jesus has a unique role to play in the kingdom of God.

Another obvious trait (at least in today's game of baseball) reflects something of the kingdom of God. To refer again to Jesus's parable, just as yeast enriches a loaf of bread, so the variety of nationalities represented in baseball enriches the sport. While by no means unique in this respect, baseball has in recent years extended its popularity in such a way that included on major league teams are, in addition to Anglo Americans and African Americans, persons from many Latin American countries, Japan, Korea, Taiwan, Canada, the Netherlands, and Australia.

Finally, there are those elements, seemingly tangential, that contribute to the sense of community for those who love the game of baseball, regardless of the nature of their involvement. For example, the seventh-inning stretch, with origins in the latter part of the nineteenth century, is accompanied today by the singing of "Take Me Out to the Ballgame." The practice of singing began when around

1970 broadcaster Harry Caray would lead the stadium fans in this song.

The song itself was written in 1908 by Jack Norworth, a vaudeville songwriter who did not attend a baseball game until June 27, 1940, when he saw the Brooklyn Dodgers defeat the Chicago Cubs, 5–4. The part sung in ballparks today is actually the refrain of a song that has two verses:

Katie Casey was baseball mad.
Had the fever and had it bad;
Just to root for the home town crew,
Ev'ry sou Katie blew.

On a Saturday, her young beau
Called to see if she'd like to go,
To see a show but Miss Kate said,
"No, I'll tell you what you can do."

[Refrain:]

Take me out to the ball game,
Take me out with the crowd,
Buy me some peanuts and crackerjacks.
I don't care if I ever get back.
So, it's root, root, root for the home team.
If they don't win, it's a shame.
And it's one, two, three strikes, you're out
At the old ball game.

Katie Casey saw all the games,
Knew the players by their first names;
Told the umpire he was wrong,
All along good and strong.

When the score was just two to two,
Katie Casey knew what to do,
Just to cheer up the boys she knew,

She made the gang sing this song:

[Refrain]

Nineteen years later the verses were revised. Katie was replaced by Nelly Kelly.[8]

Other contributions to popular culture that have to do with baseball include Terry Cashman's "Talkin' Baseball" and the Abbott and Costello comedy routine "Who's on First?" There are also recordings that have become well known because of their documentation of famous events, such as Lou Gehrig's Farewell Speech at Yankee Stadium on July 4, 1939 ("Today I consider myself the luckiest man on the face of the earth") and Russ Hodges's broadcast of Bobby Thomson's home run in the 1951 playoff game between the New York Giants and the Brooklyn Dodgers.

"The kingdom of God is like yeast that a woman took and mixed in with three measures of flour until all of it was leavened." When being baked, the yeast causes the bread to rise. It's not visible to the naked eye. And yet, without it the bread remains flat—in more than one way! The yeast gives life to the flour.

There's a sense in which all the parts of the game of baseball contribute, perhaps sometimes unwittingly, to make the game what it is—fascinating, joyful, frustrating, orderly, challenging, colorful. The parts are not interchangeable. The umpires do not announce the game. The players don't write the stories. The manager does not sell the programs. The spectators are not on the field. And, on the field, each player plays only his or her position. Each

8. http://en.wikipedia.org/wiki/Take_Me_Out_to_the_Ball_Game.

needs the others, even those on the bench or in the bullpen, to do their jobs.

God's kingdom is beyond this world. And yet, in Jesus Christ that kingdom has dawned. We are called to live in that kingdom and be its representatives in and to the world. Like a choir, we are called to sing our part and to sing it joyfully and enthusiastically. None of us can sing all the parts at the same time. But, together, all of us can contribute to the whole.

The church is called to be the provisional representation of God's kingdom in and to the world. Admittedly, it does not do that very well at times. Indeed, at times, it seems to do it very poorly. But, when guided by the Spirit of Jesus Christ, when the focus of attention is single-mindedly on the good of the whole, the church reflects the freedom and the love and grace of its head, Jesus Christ. And the kingdom of God is exhibited.

Sometimes it's hidden, like yeast in bread, but nevertheless is a witness, however seemingly small, to the goodness of God. Sometimes it's more apparent, and that, too, bears witness to God's goodness and grace.

The church could do worse than to look to the game of baseball to see ways in which it might better work together, with a single-minded purpose, as a way of reflecting and contributing to God's kingdom on earth—each of us finding our own way to do so.

5

A Game of Hard Work

(MATTHEW 20:1–16)

In his book *Men at Work: The Craft of Baseball* George Will writes: "Proof of the genius of ancient Greece is that it understood baseball's future importance. Greek philosophers considered sport a religious and civic—in a word, moral—undertaking. Sport, they said, is morally serious because mankind's noblest aim is the loving contemplation of worthy things, such as beauty and courage. By witnessing physical grace, the soul comes to understand and love beauty. Seeing people courageously and fairly helps emancipate the individual by educating his passions."[1]

It is a sign of the prowess of any athlete, in whatever sport, that he or she is able to engage with grace and apparent simplicity in something that is extraordinarily difficult. One can watch an Olympic ice skater leap and land with

1. George F. Will, *Men at Work: The Craft of Baseball* (New York: Macmillan, 1990), 2.

such ease that the viewer critiques the move as if it were the simplest act in the world—until one actually laces up some skates and discovers how difficult it is to slide along the rail hanging on for dear life, let alone to try any of the maneuvers the world sees on television.

Similarly, imagine standing in a rectangle outlined in dirt, holding a baseball bat in your hands, and facing someone sixty feet six inches away who intends to throw, with control, a small, hard ball in your direction anywhere from seventy-five to one hundred miles per hour. And you, the batter, are expected to swing the bat and hit the ball, and then to do so in a way that eight persons strategically placed in the field before you cannot reach the ball before it hits the ground. Initially, it sounds easy—until one stands in a batter's box and faces a pitcher. Then, all of a sudden, everything is different.

In his book *The Physics of Baseball*, Robert Adair quotes Rule 1.09 in the *Official Baseball Rules*, which describes the ball that's to be used in any baseball game: "The ball should be a sphere formed by yarn wound around a small sphere of cork, rubber, or similar material covered with two stripes of white horsehide or cowhide, tightly stitched together. It shall weigh not less than 5 nor more than 5¼ ounces avoirdupois and measure no less than 9 nor more than 9¼ inches in circumference."[2]

Adair goes on to describe further instructions given to the manufacturer of the baseball: "The cork-rubber composite nucleus, enclosed in rubber, is wound with 121 yards

2. Robert K. Adair, *The Physics of Baseball* (New York: Perennial, 2002) 5. Why the French term "avoirdupois" is used to indicate the weight of a baseball is unclear.

of blue-gray wool yarn, 45 yards of white wool yarn, and 150 yards of fine cotton yarn. Core and winding are enclosed by rubber cement and a two piece cowhide—horsehide before 1974—cover hand-stitched together with 216 raised red cotton stitches."[3]

While the game may seem simple, it is not easy. The catcher is the only player on the field besides the pitcher who is involved in every play. It is a difficult and demanding position. Wes Westrum, catcher for the New York Giants from 1947 to 1957, once remarked that baseball is like church: "Many attend but few understand."[4]

The whole premise of George Will's book, of course, is that, as much fun as the game of baseball is, to play the game well, even among the exceptionally talented, takes a lot of hard work. Whether it's examining the work and strategy of the manager (Tony LaRussa in Will's book) or of the pitcher, the batter, or someone in the field, one soon realizes that, as in any enterprise, the degree to which one is willing to work hard is usually the degree to which one does well. And even then, there's no guarantee of success.

For many, one of the more mystifying parables that Jesus told was the parable of the Laborers in the Vineyard (Matthew 20:1–16). Beginning in the early morning a landowner went out to hire persons to work in his vineyard. The landowner and the workers agreed on a wage for the day's work. At nine o'clock he went out again to hire more laborers, and again they agreed on a wage. At noon, three o'clock, and five o'clock the owner of the vineyard went out

3. Ibid., 5.
4. Quoted in Will, *Men at Work*, 4.

and hired workers to gather in the grapes. Each time a wage was agreed upon.

When evening came and it was time for the workers to gather to collect their wages, those who were hired last were paid first. When those who had worked all day saw that these Johnny-come-lately workers were paid what those who had been at work since early morning had agreed to be paid, naturally they figured that, because they had worked all day, they would be paid much more. Not so, according to the parable. Everyone was paid what they and the owner of the vineyard had agreed on.

Understandably, those who had labored all day were more than a little upset at the landowner. "These last worked only one hour, and you have made them equal to us who have borne the burden of the day and the scorching heat," they complained. But the landowner called them on their agreement, "Friend, I am doing you no wrong; did you not agree with me for the usual daily wage? Take what belongs to you and go; I choose to give to this last the same as I give to you. Am I not allowed to do what I choose with what belongs to me? Or are you envious because I am generous?" (Matthew 20:15). And then, Jesus concludes his words with: "So the last will be first, and the first will be last" (Matthew 20:16).

The parable is the final in a series Matthew records before Jesus enters Jerusalem as he heads towards his death. Indeed, the parable is followed by Jesus' foretelling of his imminent death and resurrection.

Several dynamics are at work here, it seems. First, clearly those who had worked the longest believed that they would receive more than those who had worked only an hour. Did Jesus aim this parable at the Pharisees, who thought that by virtue of their long and faithful allegiance to the law and its God, they stood in God's favor before anyone else? Does Jesus's description of the kingdom turn their understanding of God's love and acceptance on its head? Do those who hear the gospel with fresh ears, but who have no background in the Jewish law, find as much acceptance in the kingdom as anyone else?

A second dynamic here is the freedom of God to do as God pleases. If God makes an agreement, God is faithful in keeping that agreement, regardless of what it may look like to us. Jesus makes that clear at the end of the parable: "Am I not allowed to do what I choose with what belongs to me?" the landowner asks the laborer. The workers are not to be criticized for laboring long and hard, or for even doing so for the same wage as those who worked for a shorter period of time. The workers' error lay in presuming on the grace and generosity of the landowner. Had they not agreed to a certain wage, and had they not received the agreed-upon wage?

Robert Farrar Capon imagines the scene at the end of the day when the pay is being distributed in a graphic and modern, if humorous way:

> "Look, Pal," he tells the spokesman for all the bookkeepers who have gagged on this parable for two thousand years, "Don't give me *agita*. You agreed to $120 a day, I gave you $120 a day. Take it and get out of here before I call the cops. If I want to give some pot-head in Gucci loafers the same pay as you, so what? You're telling me I can't do what I want with my own money? I'm

> supposed to be a stinker because you got your nose out of joint? All I did was have a fun idea. I decided to put the last first and the first last to show you there are no insiders or outsiders here: when I'm happy, everybody's happy, no matter what they did or didn't do. I'm not asking you to like me, Buster; I'm telling you to enjoy me. If you want to mope, that's your business. But since the only thing it'll get you is a lousy disposition, why don't you just shut up and go into the tasting room and have yourself a free glass of Chardonnay?
>
> The choice is up to you, Friend: drink up, or get out; compliments of the house, or go to hell. Take your pick.[5]

Capon goes on to make the startling observation that "bookkeeping is the only punishable offense in the kingdom of heaven. For in that happy state, the *books* are ignored forever, and there is only the *Book* of life. And in that book, nothing stands against you."[6]

The laborers in the vineyard, like so many of us, were bookkeepers. They were keeping track of who worked for how long and, as a result, how much they should expect to be paid. After all, fair is fair. If one works longer, one should be paid more . . . except in God's kingdom where God can do whatever God wants to do. In Capon's view, "if the world could have been saved by bookkeeping, it would have been saved by Moses, not Jesus."[7]

5. Robert Farrar Capon, *The Parables of Judgment* (Grand Rapids: Eerdmans, 1989), 54.

6. Ibid., 55.

7. Ibid.

The good news is that what God wants to do is extravagant and extravagantly generous and gracious. And we, like the Pharisees, are resentful. We begrudge God's generosity . . . until we realize that we are not only as much the recipients of that generosity and grace as anyone else, but we are in as much need of that generosity and grace as anyone else.

In addition, and paradoxically, as soon as we acknowledge God's freedom to be and do whatever God desires, and as soon as we realize that in that freedom God does not require bookkeeping but offers instead gracious acceptance, we discover a new kind of freedom for ourselves. It's the kind of freedom that elicits within us a joyful response, one that cannot help but let go of all that holds us in the past, one that cannot help but want, without embarrassment or hesitation, to try to exhibit God's kingdom in all our relationships, words, and actions, one that engages in the foolishness of trying to do what God has done, namely, to love the unlovable, to accept the unacceptable, to believe the unbelievable, to think possible the impossible.

It's the kind of freedom that lives with humble confidence, a confidence that comes not from oneself but from trusting the words, "in Jesus Christ we are forgiven" and thereby released to do and be the very best one can do and be.

It's as if after one has been in prison, the doors have been unlocked, and the jailer himself has said we are free to leave. It sounds too good to be true, and yet it is true. The work that's demanded to follow Jesus Christ is difficult and challenging. Impossible, some might say. It's not easy to swim against the stream. It's difficult to put everything into one's work—whatever that work is—when others say half an effort is good enough. It's a challenge to speak out when one knows that everyone else may hold a different point of view.

The "work" that's done in response to the good news of God's love is not done to earn the favor of an angry God. Rather, the work, while demanding, is not really work at all, at least in the sense of work being tiresome, boring, and unengaging. It's a labor of love.

There's also something joyful in knowing that, with humility, one is trying to be true to a life of discipleship in everyday circumstances. Saint Augustine wrote about the city of God and the city of man. Martin Luther distinguished between the two kingdoms of God and humanity. The Apostle Paul admonishes his readers to "not be conformed to this world but be transformed by the renewal of your mind, that you may prove what is the will of God, what is good and acceptable and perfect" (Romans 12:2). While Jesus said that his kingship was not of this world (John 18:36), John also reminds us that "God so *loved* the world that God gave God's only Son that whoever believes in him should not perish but have eternal life" (John 3:16).

The truth of the matter is that we live and work in both kingdoms. They cannot be easily separated. And that's the challenge, is it not? To live and labor as citizens of the kingdom of God in another world where that kingdom is not recognized.

Baseball is a demanding sport. To play the game well, and particularly at the highest level, requires hard, disciplined work. One newspaper article reported a small part of the physical demands of the sport: "While it is well known that baseball is the slowest-paced of this country's major team sports, a minor leaguer's day goes well beyond four at-bats and nine innings mostly standing around in the field. It begins in the heat of the afternoon, taking infield, taking more swings in batting practice than anyone would ever take in a game, doing extra work in the cage, jogging in the outfield to warm up."[8]

In addition, there's work in the weight room. Then there's the job of eating healthfully to maintain one's strength, and to do so without resorting to fast-food meals on a four-figure salary. And even then, one may not make it to the major league level!

And none of this takes into account the mental discipline and concentration that are required to play the game well on a day-to-day basis.

Practice, practice, practice is the mantra for those who want to make it to Carnegie Hall. The same can be said of those who want to make it to the major leagues in baseball.

One of the frustrating aspects to the game is that there are some who seem to be blessed with more talent than others, and it seems that they don't have to work quite as hard as the others. Many stories are told of how Mickey Mantle, playing on legs that had to be taped before every game because of the constant pain he endured, played better on a consistent basis than many otherwise younger, healthier players. How many players could have made the catch Willie Mays of the New York Giants made on the fly ball to centerfield off the bat of Vic Wertz of the Cleveland Indians

8. Zachary Levine, "Needed: Bat, Ball and Buffet," *Houston Chronicle*, July 2, 2010. Online: http://www.chron.com/disp/story.mpl/sports/bb/7090966.html/.

in the 1954 World Series at the Polo Grounds? Indeed, some maintain that Mays's offensive *and* defensive abilities make him a candidate for one of the best players ever.

Clearly, natural ability is terribly important in the development of a baseball player and in determining the player's potential for reaching the major leagues. But equally clearly, even those who are naturally gifted athletically must work hard to reach and maintain a high level of performance.

Nevertheless, throughout the history of baseball there have been instances of persons with serious handicaps whose work and discipline and love for the game enabled them to play major league baseball. For instance, William Hoy played fourteen seasons in the major leagues. His debut was with the Washington Nationals in 1888. Due to childhood meningitis, he was rendered deaf and mute. And yet, he had over two thousand hits, forty home runs, 594 stolen basis, and 273 assists as an outfielder with six teams. His career batting average was .287.[9]

In the early twentieth century Mordecai "Three Finger" Brown won 239 games as a pitcher and finished a fourteen-year career with an earned-run average of 2.06. Growing up on a farm in Indiana, Brown lost his right index finger when his hand was caught in a corn grinder. While still recovering from that accident, he fell and broke the pinky and middle fingers on the same hand which grew "bent and misshapen." His "deformed hand was an impediment to gripping a baseball, but through ingenuity and practice he

9. Paul Adomites et al., *Extra Innings Baseball: All Star Stories, Stats, Lore & Legends* (Lincolnwood, IL: Publications International, 2009), 184.

developed a unique grip that produced baffling pitches with incredible movement."[10]

In a more recent time, there is the case of Jim Abbott, born in 1967 in Flint, Michigan. Abbott's right arm ended just above the wrist. He taught himself to transfer his glove from his right arm to his left hand after throwing a pitch so that he would be in a position to field the ball if necessary. At the University of Michigan his record was 26–8. He won a gold medal in the 1988 Olympics. In that same year he was drafted by the California Angels and in 1989 had a record of 12–12 with the Angels. In 1993 he pitched a no-hitter for the New York Yankees.

None of this takes into account the mental aspect of the game; that is to say, not simply the rules of the game, but how the game is played in certain situations. And when the situations change, the way the game is played may change as well. For example, when should the cut-off man take the throw from the outfielder, and when should he let it go through? The answers depend on the situation: Where is the runner? How fast is the runner? What's the score? Are there other runners on base?

How does one become a batter who strikes out very seldom? How does one become a good base stealer? How does one learn the intricacies of the game, such as when to throw a fastball and when to throw a slider, and to whom? How does one learn for which hitters or in which situations he should play close to the line at third base, and for which hitters or in which situations he should play ten feet off the line? How does a pitcher know when to field a bunt and when to let the catcher or one of the other fielders take it?

10. Ibid., 185.

The answer to these questions is the same: practice, practice, practice; work, work, work. But all the practice and all the work are intended to make one a better player. It doesn't always follow that the more one works at something, the greater the guarantee that one will be better than other players. One practices and works to improve one's game. Period. One practices and works out of love for the game. Period.

George Will observes that "the best players pay the most attention to baseball's parts." He then goes on to tell a well-known story about the great Yankee player Joe DiMaggio: "Frank Crosetti, a Yankee coach, saw every game DiMaggio played and never saw him thrown out going from first to third. When DiMaggio was asked why he placed such a high value on excellence he said, 'There is always some kid who may be seeing me for the first or last time. I owe him my best.'"[11]

Will also points to another example of the kind of excellence demanded by good baseball players.

> It is the everydayness of baseball that demands of the player a peculiar equilibrium, a balance of relaxation and concentration. One afternoon, during Andre Dawson's 1987 MVP season, he was in right field in Wrigley Field and the Cubs were clobbering the Astros, 11–1. In the top of the sixth inning Dawson ran down a foul fly, banging into the brick wall that is right next to the foul line. In the seventh inning he charged and made a sliding catch on a low line drive that otherwise would have been an unimportant

11. Will, *Men at Work*, 325.

> single. When asked after the game why he would risk injuries in those situations when the outcome of the game was not in doubt, Dawson replied laconically, "Because the ball was in play." Dawson probably found the question unintelligible. The words and syntax were clear enough but the questioner obviously was oblivious to the mental (and moral) world of a competitor like Dawson.[12]

Will also observes that there is dignity in "honest mediocrity." If one is doing one's best, that is all that is asked. Even if others are better players, there is dignity for everyone. Indeed, there's a kind of heroism in anyone who plays the game with passion, integrity, and care, regardless of the level of the player's skill.

Something similar can be said of those who seek to live as representatives of God's kingdom in the world. They do so passionately, but also with humility. They do so unpretentiously, knowing that they are only laborers, but they do so with thoughtfulness and integrity. They are willing to be anonymous, but they give everything they have to the work because they care about the work. They find tremendous satisfaction in the work because they have found true freedom in forgetting about themselves and binding themselves to the landowner.

"So the last will be first, and the first will be last"—in the kingdom of God.

12. Ibid., 328.

6

A Game of Unexpected Heroes

(MATTHEW 13:31–32)

> The kingdom of heaven is like a mustard seed that someone took and sowed in his field; it is the smallest of all the seeds, but when it has grown it is the greatest of shrubs and becomes a tree, so that the birds of the air come and make nests in its branches.

THIS parable is told in the midst of a whole series of parables in Matthew 13, most of which are agricultural in nature, and all of which have to do with the kingdom of heaven. Often the parables Jesus tells have to do with the value, at least from God's point of view, of something others might consider small, minor, insignificant. He takes the ordinary and mundane, and points us to its power and importance.

Such is the case with the parable of the mustard seed. The tiniest of seeds, one mustard seed is not much larger than a couple grains of salt, something to which, by itself, few of us would pay any mind. And yet, in this briefest of parables, Jesus compares the kingdom of heaven to it because when fully grown, it becomes a tree and provides a home for birds.

Unexpected heroes. We come across a lot of unexpected characters in Scripture who turn out to be used by God for God's purposes. Whether or not we would call them heroes is another matter. Or, if we do call them heroes, we must be clear about our definition of that word.

In their book *Heroism and the Christian Life: Reclaiming Excellence*, Brian Hook and R. R. Reno examine the idea of the "hero" in Homer's *Iliad*, Plato's view of Socrates in *The Apology*, Virgil's *Aeneid*, the depiction of Jesus in the Gospels and of Paul in early Christianity, the works of Spenser and Milton, and, finally, of Camus and Bonhoeffer in the twentieth century.[1] Their argument is that while the Christian life of discipleship is not heroic in the same way that Achilles or Socrates might be heroic, it is a life of self-emptying (*kenosis*, from Philippians 2:7) that demands standards of excellence in living. It is the kind of life that, on their own, persons called by God for God's own purposes would never have chosen for themselves. And yet, it is the kind of life that, in retrospect, they would never have given up for anything else.

One can think of biblical characters the course of whose lives were unalterably changed, not by their own choice, but by God's call. Would Abram have ever insisted that he and Sarah leave their own homeland of Ur and

1. Brian S. Hook and R. R. Reno, *Heroism and the Christian Life: Reclaiming Excellence* (Louisville: Westminster John Knox, 2000).

travel thousands of miles to a land unknown to them or their ancestors (Genesis 12)? Would Moses, on his own initiative, have ever left Edom to return to Egypt, where he could have been found guilty of murder, to lead a bunch of slaves in rebellion against the pharaoh without God's call to him from a burning bush (Exodus 3)? Would Isaiah, on his own, have ever prophesied against the southern kingdom of Judah had he never experienced God's presence and call in the temple "in the year that King Uzziah died" (Isaiah 6)? Would Saul have ever, on his own, reached the decision that the way of those Christians whom he helped persecute was truly the right way, had he not encountered the risen Christ on the road to Damascus (Acts 9:1–24)?

If one went through the names listed in "the roll call of faith" in Hebrews 11, one could safely say that whatever "heroic" deeds these individuals may have accomplished, none of them would have considered themselves heroes, and certainly none of them would have done what they did on their own. Indeed, most people would consider them unlikely candidates for the tasks they accomplished.

And the same might also be said of many who demonstrated extraordinary courage in the face of the Nazi threat in the middle of the twentieth century. Who would have imagined that a small Reformed congregation in southern France, led by a courageous pastor, Andre Trocme, would be the ones who provided shelter and safety to hundreds of Jews fleeing Nazi persecution in World War II?[2]

2. Cf. Philip P. Haillie's account of this remarkable community in his book, *Lest Innocent Blood Be Shed: The Story of the Village of Le Chambon and How Goodness Happened There* (New York: Harper Perennial, 1994).

Similarly, Oskar Schindler, a German who had had very little to do with the church, and Varian Fry, an American living in Marseilles, France, were most unlikely candidates to demonstrate the kind of courage needed to protect Jews who otherwise would have died at the hands of the Nazis.[3]

Many who participated in the civil rights movement in the 1950s and 1960s in this country might be considered unlikely candidates for a hero's medal, but these demonstrated courage and excellence in their response to a call to labor for justice. Consider Fannie Lou Hamer, resident of Ruleville, Mississippi, who left "the cotton fields of the Delta in 1962 to 'work for Jesus' in civil rights activism."[4] In 1964 she represented the Mississippi Freedom Democratic Party at the Democratic National Convention in Atlantic City, New Jersey, seeking to unseat the all-white state delegation. Of Mrs. Hamer, Charles Marsh writes: "As a member of the Student Nonviolent Coordinating Committee and a courageous leader in voter registration and grass-roots political organizing, Mrs. Hamer gave eloquent witness to a liberating, reconciling faith, shaped by a skillful blending of African American hymnody and spirituality, prophetic religion, and an indefatigable belief in Jesus as friend and deliverer of the poor."[5]

3. The popular movie *Schindler's List* is based on the book by Thomas Keneally (New York: Simon & Schuster, 1994). Sheila Isenberg has written about Varian Fry's life in Marseilles during World War II in her book, *A Hero of Our Own: The Story of Varian Fry* (New York: Random House, 2001).

4. Charles Marsh, *God's Long Summer: Stories of Faith and Civil Rights* (Princeton: Princeton University Press, 1997), 4.

5. Ibid., 5.

Mrs. Hamer had not only been beaten as she sought to register African Americans to vote, but she had also been sterilized when she went to the hospital to have a small uterine tumor removed. She woke up after the surgery to discover that the doctors had performed a hysterectomy. Apparently, no one had informed her that this might be a possibility.[6]

Living in poverty all her life, even up to the time of her death in 1977, this woman gave voice to a theology that informed and shaped much of the civil rights movement. Marsh describes it as

> a distinctive Christian discourse, evangelical in the most vigorous sense of the term, a robust and disciplined love of Jesus of Nazareth, of the whole scandalous story of his life, death, and resurrection. At the same time, her love was a great big love, open to anyone who cared for the weak and the poor. Was this not the message of the Gospel? She believed it was . . . Jesus was God's son, sacrificed on the bloody cross for the sins of the world, raised miraculously from the dead on the third day, coming again in glory to judge the world and gather home his children. But Jesus was also a "radical" and a "militant," and were he living in the Delta in 1964, he would be branded a "red." Christ was a real revolutionary, "out there where it's happening."[7]

Then there's the unlikely candidate for a hero or a saint in the person of a white housewife from Detroit, Michigan,

6. Ibid., 20.
7. Ibid., 45.

who, upon seeing on television what was going on in Alabama in 1965, decided that she had to go and volunteer to help register African Americans to vote. Following the march from Selma to Montgomery, led by Martin Luther King Jr., Viola Liuzzo was driving an African American civil rights worker from Selma to Montgomery when she was shot and killed by a person in another car. This person was later identified as a member of the Ku Klux Klan.[8]

Dozens of other examples of "mustard seeds" that grew into magnificent trees by virtue of their own witness to the gospel, even if unwittingly, could be offered from any and all generations. Many, if not most, of these persons were not thrust into critical situations of their own choosing. They had seen a need, and they responded.

Baseball has had its share of unexpected heroes. Mention has been made of Don Larsen, the only pitcher to hurl a perfect game in the World Series. It was the fifth game of the 1956 World Series when Larsen, playing for the New York Yankees, faced the minimum of twenty-seven Brooklyn Dodgers hitters over nine innings, and the Yankees won the game 2–0 and went on to win the series, four games to three.

One might expect that those who have pitched in the major leagues would include some of the best pitchers in the game. Indeed, such greats as Cy Young, Sandy Koufax, Jim "Catfish" Hunter, Dennis Martinez, David Cone, and Randy Johnson have all been credited with perfect games. It's also noteworthy that many others considered to be among the elite pitchers of the game never pitched perfect

8. Al Kuettner, *March to a Promised Land: The Civil Rights Files of a White Reporter, 1952–1968* (Sterling, VA: Capital, 2006), 149–50.

games (for example, Christy Mathewson, Dizzy Dean, Whitey Ford, Warren Spahn, and Tom Seaver).

Larsen's 81–91 win-loss record is indicative of the fact that some perfect games have been pitched by those with less than stellar careers. The last person to pitch a perfect game in the major leagues before Larsen was Charlie Robertson. Robertson accomplished this feat for the Chicago White Sox on April 30, 1922, against the Detroit Tigers in Detroit. What's remarkable was that this was only Robertson's fifth major league start. A native of Texas, Robertson attended Austin College for two years (1917–1919) before signing with the White Sox.

Robertson's professional baseball career lasted until 1928. After playing for the White Sox through the 1925 season, he went on to play for the St. Louis Browns (1926) and the Boston Braves (1927 and 1928). His career win-loss record was a less than sterling 49–80.

But on one Sunday afternoon in Detroit the twenty-six-year-old rookie from Nocona, Texas, faced the minimum of twenty-seven batters and managed to get them all out. Ty Cobb, the player-manager for the Tigers, protested vehemently throughout the game that Robertson was doctoring the ball with some kind of grease. The men in blue were never able to find any such evidence.

Players who get game-winning hits or walk-off home runs are rightfully acknowledged and feted. However, often such hits would not have received any attention had they not have been preceded by other crucial hits or plays in other innings.

For example, Bill Mazeroski's dramatic walk-off home run in the bottom of the ninth inning of Game Seven, winning the 1960 World Series for the Pittsburgh Pirates over the New York Yankees, will be remembered by many for a long time. However, in the eighth inning Hal Smith, a reserve catcher replacing Smoky Burgess and batting for his only time in the game, capped a five-run rally by hitting a three-run home run to put the Pirates ahead, 9–7. In the top of the ninth inning the Yankees scored two runs to tie the game, thus setting the stage for Mazeroski's game- and Series-winning home run. While Bill Mazeroski will be a name etched in the memory of many for his hit, it is unlikely that Hal Smith is as well remembered.

In a similarly dramatic World Series, in 1988 the Los Angeles Dodgers faced the heavily favored Oakland Athletics. Dodger left-fielder Kirk Gibson had injured both legs in the National League Championship Series against the New York Mets. In addition, he had a stomach virus and was not expected to play in Game One.

Entering the bottom of the ninth inning, the Dodgers trailed, 4–3. Starter Dave Stewart was replaced by closer Dennis Eckersley to get the last three outs. Eckersley got Mike Scioscia to pop out and Jeff Hamilton to strike out. He then pitched around and walked pinch-hitter Mike Davis, thinking he was going to face David Anderson, a righthanded hitter, who was in the on-deck circle. Although Gibson was hurt, he was in the clubhouse receiving treatment for his injured legs. He sent word to manager Tommy Lasorda that he was available to pinch-hit if he were needed.

With Davis on first base, Lasorda sent for Gibson, and he hobbled up to the plate. After working the count to three balls and two strikes, Gibson lofted Eckersley's next pitch over the right field fence, giving the Dodgers a 5–4 victory in Game One. They went on to win the Series, four games to one.

The image of Gibson hobbling around the bases, excitedly pumping his right arm, remains etched in the memories of those who witnessed that dramatic event, either in person or on television. However, the game would probably never have reached that point had not Mickey Hatcher, Gibson's replacement in left field, who had hit only one home run all year, connected on a two-run home run off Stewart in the first inning. Incidentally, Hatcher hit another home run in the fifth and final game of the Series.

There were many stars in the Negro Leagues who went unnoticed until Branch Rickey and Jackie Robinson broke the color barrier in 1948 (which will be covered in the next chapter). Josh Gibson, Satchel Paige, Buck O'Neil, and Cool Papa Bell are only a few names that come to mind. Some who played in the Negro Leagues also became stars in the major leagues: Hank Aaron, Willie Mays, Roy Campanella, Larry Doby, and Monte Irvin, for example.

Yet one who receives little attention but who had a remarkable career was Larry Brown. Brown was born in Pratt City, Alabama, and began playing for the Birmingham Black Barons when he was seventeen years old. A catcher who reportedly threw out Ty Cobb five consecutive times in an exhibition game, he gained a reputation as an "iron man" behind the plate and one of the finest catchers to play the game. In 1930, while playing for the New York Lincoln Giants, Brown is said to have caught 234 games (a normal season today is 162 games) He led his teams to three championships, and he played in six Negro All-Star Games. And yet, his name is not often mentioned with the other greats of the game.

In the game of baseball there are times when a player is called upon to sacrifice himself in order to advance a runner, so that a team will have a better chance of scoring. Rarely do the little things like that show up in the box score or in the story of the game. And yet, without them the team's chances of winning diminish significantly. Some of the unexpected heroes are those who do the little things that lead to the bigger things. They may not have the highest batting average or the lowest earned-run average or the fastest legs, but they contribute something of significance to the team.

Jesus's parable of the mustard seed reflects the way he looked at and treated others. He stopped to heal a blind beggar when everyone else thought the beggar was not worth the attention (Mark 10:46–52). He pointed his disciples to the poor widow and her offering to the temple treasury when no one else would likely have noticed the significance of her contribution (Luke 21:1–4). He went to eat in the home of tax collector Zacchaeus, a man despised by other Jews for his complicity with the Roman authorities (Luke 19:1–10). He made conversation with a Samaritan woman at Jacob's Well—something frowned upon by Jewish leaders (John 4:1–26). He told the parable of the lost sheep to the Pharisees and the scribes (Luke 15:1–7) as a way of indicating that no one is beyond God's love and God's reach, even when the other ninety-nine sheep are in the fold.

Mustard seeds all, and yet, their lives were transformed by Jesus. Jesus looked beyond the obvious, beyond their "smallness" and saw opportunities for his kingdom to be proclaimed and celebrated.

7

A Game That Reflects Society

(MATTHEW 13:1–9)

SPORTS, while a form of entertainment, are also part of everyday life. Because it is played on an everyday basis during the season, baseball seems to carry with it more of that everyday life than most other sports. That may be why many issues in the everyday world seem to carry over into baseball.

Although much too late, baseball integrated well before other professional sports. The issue of free agency and having the right to form a union and enter into a collective bargaining agreement with the team owners took place in baseball before other sports. While it may not have been unique to baseball, the social unrest in this country in the 1960s and 1970s had an effect on baseball, perhaps more so because of its everyday nature.

Even if sports in general, and baseball in particular, are considered part of the entertainment world to which many repair to escape, if only for a few hours, the tensions and headaches of the workaday world, the world of baseball still reflects our world (at least in terms of wins and losses, hits and outs, terrific plays and errors) in a way that many find gratifying. Except for the catcher, who wears a face-mask, players wear only a batting helmet and a glove for protection. Otherwise, players are simply out in the field playing a simple game that demands excellence if it is to be satisfying at all.

And yet a mythology surrounds baseball. David Halberstam maintains that the slowness of the game (especially compared to professional basketball and football), combined with the fact that baseball players are not always the best athletes, demands mythology:

> Baseball is, I think, the sport in which illusion and reality are furthest apart. Its dependence upon statistics proves its need for mythology; the performance is not fulfilling enough; it must be shown in quantified heroics, records to be set and broken, new myths and heroes to replace the old . . . The height of the mound is to be tampered with if the records slip and there aren't enough .300 hitters around. A team with two .300 hitters is a team with heroes, but what myths can spring up about a .275 hitter? This, I think, was the dilemma for Roger Maris in 1961 and his remarkable unpopularity. He was breaking the record of one great mythological figure, the cripple-loving Babe, which was bad enough, but what was worse, he was doing it when the fans, led by the New York sportswriters and

> media, had been carefully indoctrinated to think that if the record fell it should go to Mantle.[1]

But then something happens to demythologize these heroes, and we can no longer enjoy the illusion and the myth that some of these players are some kind of superheroes. Not only are some of their flaws revealed, but they are shown to live in the same world the rest of us do.

> A sower went out to sow. And as he sowed, some seeds fell on the path, and the birds came and ate them up. Other seeds fell on rocky ground, where they did not have much soil, and they sprang up quickly, since they had no depth of soil. But when the sun rose, they were scorched; and since they had no root, they withered away. Other seeds fell among thorns, and the thorns grew up and choked them. Other seeds fell on good soil and brought forth grain, some a hundredfold, some sixty, some thirty. (Matthew 13:1–5,7–9, NRSV)

The seed that fell on good soil took root and produced good, healthy grain. And, apparently, it did so right beside, or at least very near, rocky ground and thorny ground. And somehow most of the seeds that fell on good soil managed not to be devoured by birds.

The good seed was not immune to the elements that could have harmed it, nor was it likely to be uninfluenced by nearby rocky soil or thorns. But it did, nonetheless, fall

1. David Halberstam, "Baseball and the National Mythology," in *Everything They Had: Sports Writing from David Halberstam*, ed. Glenn Stout (New York: Hyperion, 2008), 66.

into good soil and produce good and healthy grain—within an environment that included all kinds of less healthy soil.

Following Matthew's account of this parable, at the request of his disciples Jesus explains the meaning of the parable:

> When any one hears the word of the kingdom and does not understand it, the evil one comes and snatches away what is sown in his heart; this is what was sown along the path. As for what was sown on rocky ground, this is he who hears the word and immediately receives it with joy; yet he has no root in himself, but endures for a while, and when tribulation or persecution arises on account of the word, immediately he falls away. As for what was sown among thorns, this is he who hears the word, but the cares of the world and the delight in riches choke the word, and it proves unfruitful. As for what was sown on good soil, this is he who hears the word and understands it; he indeed bears fruit, and yields, in one case a hundredfold, in another sixty, and in another thirty. (Matthew 13:19–23)

What fascinates about this kingdom parable is that the kingdom grows beside and in the middle of those elements that might inhibit it: weeds, thorns, rocks, clay, limestone, poison ivy, too many trees that prevent sunshine from reaching the soil. What is equally intriguing is that Jesus does not say that all those things that keep the seed from taking root should be removed, but rather he focuses on the seed that does find good soil.

We are reminded of words from Isaiah 43:

> Do not remember the former things
> or consider the things of old.
> I am about to do a new thing;
> now it springs forth, do you not perceive it?"
> (vv. 18–19b, NRSV).

Jesus's response to the Pharisees' question about when the kingdom of God was coming also comes to mind: "The kingdom of God is not coming with things that can be observed; nor will they say, 'Look, here it is!' or 'There it is!' For, in fact, the kingdom of God is among you (Luke 17:20–21, NRSV).

According to Jesus, the kingdom, while not always visible or even discernible in the world, is in our midst. Even though the seed that falls into good soil is surrounded by weeds and thorns and rocks, nevertheless it grows in the midst of those things.

Paul's way of putting it is found in his letter to the Romans: "Do not be conformed to this world, but be transformed by the renewing of your minds, so that you may discern what is the will of God—what is good and acceptable and perfect" (12:2, NRSV). The tension between being in the world and yet also being representatives of God's kingdom to the world has always existed, and that's a tension with which those who claim the title "disciple of Jesus Christ" must constantly struggle.

In 1945 Branch Rickey, the general manager of the Brooklyn Dodgers, signed Jackie Robinson to a minor league contract to play for the Montreal Royals. Two years later, on April 15, 1947, Robinson played his first game for the Dodgers, an event that broke the color line in major league baseball. Larry Doby would soon follow in the

American League, signing with the Cleveland Indians on July 4, 1947. Two years later Robinson, Don Newcombe, and Roy Campanella, all from the Dodgers, made the National League All-Star team, while Doby made the American League All-Stars. Monte Irvin, whom Rickey had approached in 1945 about becoming the first black player in the major leagues, but who was rejected because Rickey thought he had not developed enough since leaving the armed forces, was eventually signed by the New York Giants in 1949.

Rickey, a devout Methodist layman, graduated from Ohio Wesleyan University in 1906. He earned a law degree from Ohio State University. Long before the 1954 *Brown v. Board of Education* Supreme Court decision that made desegregation the law of the land, Rickey not only saw the injustice of racial discrimination and segregated baseball leagues but was determined to do something about it. Racial segregation had been part of the major leagues ever since the late nineteenth century, when Cap Anson, a star for the Chicago Cubs, worked to keep the color line clear and firm.

In his biography of Branch Rickey, Lee Lowenfish writes of Rickey's embarrassment over racial discrimination in a country that had just fought a war "against an enemy who believed in the superiority of the white Aryan race."[2] At the same time, Lowenfish notes, while he was disgusted with racial discrimination in any form, "Rickey remained

2. Lee Lowenfish, *Branch Rickey: Baseball's Ferocious Gentleman* (Lincoln: University of Nebraska Press, 2007), 351.

a very conservative man, fearful of any leftist, collectivist, or—worst of all— Communist agitation of the race issue."[3]

Black major league teams would rent and play on major league fields when the white teams were on the road or during the offseason. Economically, it was in the white owners' best interest not to integrate the major leagues. Moreover, most of the white owners were not in favor of integration anyway. Baseball commissioner Kenesaw Landis was in no hurry to have black players sign with white teams.

Nevertheless, during World War II there were teams that explored the possibility of signing black players. The Pittsburgh Pirates and the Washington Senators looked at such players as Satchel Paige, Josh Gibson, and Walter "Buck" Leonard, among others, but decided not to pursue them.

Rickey, however, saw the talent in the Negro leagues as talent to be cultivated and, eventually, to be signed to the major leagues. He had both a competitive and an economic motive, for he believed that, with talented black players to go with talented white players, the Dodgers would compete consistently for the pennant.

But Lowenfish observes that there was an additional motive behind Rickey's desire to revolutionize major league baseball by signing black players, namely, "a genuine Wesleyan Methodist conscience at work. One of his favorite litanies went, 'The Negro has never been really free in this country. Legally free since the Civil War yes, but not politically or socially free, and never morally free."[4]

3. Ibid.

4. Ibid., 354.

He lauded the achievements of Jesse Owens at the 1936 Olympics in Berlin, Germany. He followed the boxer Joe Louis, as he worked his way towards becoming heavyweight champion of the world by defeating his white opponents. But because baseball required working as a team member as well as excelling as an individual, Rickey's work was made even more difficult. College football had been integrated since the 1920s, and that was one place to start. At UCLA there were three black athletes who started in the backfield. One was named Jackie Robinson.

Rickey was not interested in signing just any black player. The person had to be not only talented but intelligent and of the right disposition; that is, he had to be able to stand up to the taunts, epithets, and attacks that would surely be hurled at him. He had friends scout various players and report to him secretly. Rickey knew that if the wrong player were chosen to be first, integration in the big leagues could be set back significantly.

Inviting Dodger broadcaster Red Barber into his confidence, Rickey shared his secret plan to sign a black ballplayer. Barber, a son of the South and native of Columbus, Mississippi, was not all that enthusiastic, and indeed seriously considered resigning. After discussing the matter with his wife, Lyla, and sleeping on it, Barber decided he could report the games as he saw them without prejudice. He was reminded, according to Lowenfish, "of the passage in *The Book of Common Prayer*, a late-sixteenth-century work from Elizabethan England that was one of his and Branch Rickey's favorite sources for inspiration: 'and has opened the eyes of the mind to behold things invisible and unseen.'"[5]

Jackie Robinson played his entire career for the Brooklyn Dodgers, from 1947 to 1956. He was elected to the National League All-Stars every year from 1949 to 1954. In 1949 he received the National League's Most Valuable Player award. He was elected into the Hall of Fame in Cooperstown in 1962. He died in 1972 at the age of fifty-three years.

Branch Rickey had served as business manager of the St. Louis Cardinals before the title "general manager" had been coined. One of his notable innovations was the establishment of a farm system. From St. Louis he went to Brooklyn where he served as "president and general manager" of the Dodgers. Not only did he break the color barrier in the major leagues by signing Jackie Robinson, but he developed the Dodger farm system, which laid the groundwork for future World Series contenders. Eventually, Rickey went to Pittsburgh where once again he prepared the foundation for a future world champion (1960).

Rickey was elected to the baseball Hall of Fame in 1967. He died at the age of eighty-four years in 1965.

In sum, during the mid-twentieth century, in many respects baseball reflected American society in terms of its racial segregation and its prejudices. But in another respect, due to the vision and courage of Branch Rickey, baseball proved to be ahead of society by its willingness to take the risk of insisting on integration. Sometimes the seed falls on fertile soil.

5. Ibid., 361.

What's fascinating is that Rickey, Robinson, and the major leagues all preceded this country, other sports, and the church in possessing the courage to desegregate. The convergence of one man's taking seriously his understanding of the gospel with the availability of a superior athlete, who was not only gifted physically, but who had the character and the temperament to overcome all the racist obstacles that might have been too much for most other candidates made it possible.

Ironically, though baseball broke the color line before other professional sports, and certainly before the country's laws were changed to break that barrier, race remains an issue in major league baseball. While the number of African Americans has soared in professional basketball and football, the numbers have declined in baseball. Furthermore, African Americans in baseball have found the path to executive positions more difficult than in other sports; here again baseball mirrors society in many respects.

In other ways too baseball reflects issues faced by society in general. Baseball players have been no more immune to the temptations of drug use than the rest of the world. Steve Howe and Darrel Strawberry are only two players whose careers were seriously affected, and eventually cut short, by drug use.

In the late 1990s and early 2000s some players tried to gain a competitive edge by using steroids. The drive and the pressure to excel began to resemble similar pressures in the business world where it also was not uncommon to find drug use (albeit not necessarily of steroids).

In his book *The Bronx Is Burning*, Jonathan Mahler examines New York City in 1977: its political life, its social life, and the Yankees' World Series victory over the Los Angeles Dodgers. The win over the Dodgers, four games to two, featured Reggie Jackson's three home runs in Game Six. This was also the season when Jackson got into a heated and dramatic argument with manager Billy Martin in the dugout, which was part of the Saturday-afternoon live televised coverage.

Baseball takes place in the context of society and social and political events and developments. Those who play baseball are part of society and cannot help but be affected by world events, especially those that are momentous. Whether the events revolve around race or political contests or the search for a serial killer named Son of Sam, who terrorized New York denizens and who was finally caught and identified as David Berkowitz, the game of baseball continued.[6]

Similarly, the Christian life cannot be separated from the world in which we live. It is no accident that in telling the story of Jesus's birth, Luke begins by reminding readers that Augustus was emperor, and that he had commanded that a census be taken, and that Quirinius was governor of Syria. The region in which Jesus lived was occupied by Roman soldiers and officials. He was tried and convicted by a Roman official. How does one separate the life of discipleship from the world, or society, in which one lives?

"A sower went out to sow . . ." The kingdom emerges from fertile soil, soil that has been carefully cultivated. But its growth occurs in the midst of weeds, rocks, and thorns. Our hope and prayer is that the kingdom will influence them more than they will influence the kingdom. Similarly,

6. Jonathan Mahler, *The Bronx is Burning: 1977, Baseball, Politics, and the Battle for the Soul of a City* (New York: Picador, 2005),

when played right, baseball can occasionally, as in the case of Rickey and Robinson, bear witness to the society that surrounds it rather than always being influenced by it.

8

Communion of Saints

(HEBREWS 12:1–2)

THE Hall of Fame. Cooperstown, New York. To have a place there is every player's aspiration. To be able to walk among the greats who are honored in that museum is every baseball fan's dream.

For many it takes on a religious aura. Even the president of the Hall, Jeff Idelson, has been quoted as saying, "Since its founding by Stephen C. Clark and its opening a museum in 1939, the Baseball Hall of Fame has always been the definitive repository of baseball's important relics and the museum has always drawn national attention as a showcase for the game's sacred past."[1]

The stories and statistics behind the engraved countenances of the players elected to the Hall, as well as the bats and gloves that Hall of Famers used, and the uniforms

1. Quoted in Zev Chafets, *Cooperstown Confidential: Heroes, Rogues, and the Inside Story of the Baseball Hall of Fame* (New York: Bloomsbury, 2009), 4.

they wore, no doubt all contribute to a sense of awe and appreciation for the talent, work, and accomplishments they represent. As a viewer might in any museum, one imagines being present when the items behind the glass case were actually used.

The National Baseball Hall of Fame and Museum first opened in June 1939. However, the first election of persons to fill the Hall of Fame was held in 1936. Five players mustered the required 75 percent of the votes: Ty Cobb, Babe Ruth, Honus Wagner, Christy Mathewson, and Walter Johnson. By the time the Hall opened, twenty-six members had been enshrined.

Other than needing to receive 75 percent of the votes cast, players must have at least ten years of major league experience, have been retired for at least five years if living, or deceased for at least six months. In addition, a screening committee determines the eligibility of players by using additional criteria: a player's record, playing ability, integrity, sportsmanship, and character. Voting is by the Baseball Writers Association of America. As of 2010, a total of 292 individuals had been inducted, including 232 players, twenty managers, nine umpires, and thirty-one pioneers and executives.

In 1961 Jackie Robinson was the first African American player to be elected to the Hall of Fame. Between 1971 and 1977, a special Negro Leagues Committee inducted nine players from the Negro leagues. Since 1977, the Veterans Committee, a body made up of former players, considered players from the Negro leagues and chose nine more individuals. In 2005, the Hall of Fame formed a Committee on African American Baseball. That body elected seventeen persons from the Negro Leagues and earlier, nineteenth-century teams.[2]

Whether it's such well-known names as Cy Young, Dizzy Dean, Joe DiMaggio, Ted Williams, Stan Musial, Monte Irvin, Mickey Mantle, Ernie Banks, Willie Mays, Roberto Clemente, Joe Morgan, Rod Carew, George Brett, and Andre Dawson; or lesser-known persons from the nineteenth century, such as Old Hoss Radbourn, Dan Brouthers, Mickey Welch, John Clarkson, Ed Delahanty, and Jesse Burkett, all are part of the pantheon of players who played the game, played it well, and played it with passion and joy.

But behind that grand collection of outstanding players, coaches, umpires, and executives are thousands of others who loved the game and participated in it with dedication and joyful abandon—not as skilled, perhaps, but no less enthusiastic about the game itself.

One should not suffer the illusion, however, that those who are in the Hall of Fame somehow were perfect, or even qualitatively superior in any moral sense. In his book *Cooperstown Confidential*, Zev Chafets reminds us that many players enter the Hall of Fame in spite of questionable character and integrity. For example, Cap Anson, who played in the 1890s and was inducted into the Hall of Fame in 1939, was a leader among those determined to keep major league baseball segregated.[3]

2. "List of members of the Baseball Hall of Fame." *Wikipedia*. Online: http://enwikipedia.org/wiki/National_Baseball_Hall_of_Fame_and_Museum/.

3. Zev Chafets, *Cooperstown Confidential: Heroes, Rogues, and the Inside Story of the Baseball Hall of Fame* (New York: Bloomsbury,

Ty Cobb, among the first to be elected to the Hall, earned a reputation for not only playing hard but also dirty. Babe Ruth, credited with returning baseball to popularity after the 1919 Black Sox scandal, and the single-season home run leader until 1961 (when Roger Maris broke that record with sixty-one) as well as the career home run leader until 1974 (when Hank Aaron broke that record by hitting his 714th home run), was notorious for drinking and carousing.

Then, there are those who, despite excellent statistics, are not in the Hall of Fame because of their questionable character and activities. Pete Rose, all-time leader in career hits with 4,256 as well as at-bats, outs, and games played, was banned from the game by commissioner Bart Giamatti when it was discovered that Rose had bet on games as a player and as a manager.

Many argue that Shoeless Joe Jackson should be in the Hall of Fame because he was acquitted by a jury of participating with his Chicago White Sox teammates in throwing the World Series against the Cincinnati Reds in 1919. Jackson, along with those who confessed to the scandal, was banned from baseball for life by the newly appointed commissioner, Kennesaw "Mountain" Landis.[4]

In the late 1990s and early 2000s, the use of illegal steroids (such as human-growth hormones) has threatened to keep otherwise certain Hall of Famers from induction. Some who have been accused of steroid use include Mark Maguire, Barry Bonds, and Roger Clemens.

2009), 56.

4. Donald Gropman, *The True Story of Shoeless Joe Jackson and the 1919 World Series* (New York: Lynx, 1988), 159.

> Therefore, since we are surrounded by so great a cloud of witnesses, let us also lay aside every weight and the sin that clings so closely, and let us run with perseverance the race that is set before us, looking to Jesus the pioneer and perfecter of our faith, who for the sake of the joy that was set before him endured the cross, disregarding its shame, and has taken his seat at the right hand of the throne of God. (Hebrews 12:1–2)

These powerful and inspiring words serve as a reminder to each generation that they are called to live the Christian life with joy, with passion, committed with every fiber of their being to Jesus Christ, "the pioneer and perfecter of our faith." Furthermore, those who have gone before, those who have run and completed their race, are in the stands cheering us on, offering encouragement and support.

This image of a stadium in which athletes are competing in a track meet is easily transferable to most any other sport or venue, including baseball. Regardless of how talented one is or is not, imagine actually being on the field with others playing baseball. Now imagine the fans in the stands cheering not only for you but for everyone on the field, cheering for everyone to have fun, to play with joyful abandon, to give it one's very best—not because it's a competition, but rather for the joy of the game. It's demanding, and requires our best effort, regardless of what that looks like.

We follow in the footsteps of those who have gone before us. And yet, we are also making our own mark. But all of us, past and present, are participants in, and citizens of the kingdom. It's been said that, if we are able to have a vision of the future, it is only because we stand on the shoulders of those who have gone before us.

As citizens of the kingdom, there's a certain equality that applies to everyone. The focus of attention is not on who's in and who's out, or who won and who lost, or on any of the competitive edges that seem to consume so many of us. Rather, the focus of attention is on Jesus Christ, the one who always goes before us, and yet the one who is always in our midst. The focus of attention is on Jesus Christ, the one who in perfect obedience to the Father, gave himself up for us on the cross that we might discover the extent of God's irresistible grace and the true joy and freedom that come with being enveloped in that grace.

Discipleship is not a chore but a labor of love. It is a labor because it is not easy. It is perhaps the most difficult endeavor one can engage in. But it's done with love because there is nothing more exciting, challenging, life-transforming. The goal is not happiness or self-fulfillment. On the contrary, the goal is death to one's self and one's own motives, and discovering new life, resurrection life, a life we could never have imagined, in him who "for the sake of the joy that was set before him endured the cross, disregarding its shame, and has taken his seat at the right hand of the throne of God" (Hebrews 12:2, NRSV).

Those that have gone before us and are now among that great cloud of witnesses watch with great interest and intensity, cheering us on, as we, who are now on the field, play the game to the best of our ability. Some may be more gifted than others. Some may appear to be only average. Some may not play well at all. But we are all in the game doing the best we can—not competing against each other but encouraging each other, even cheering for each other, playing the game with joy and trying to bring honor to the game, attempting to be the best representatives of the game to everyone else that we can be.

One verse in William Walsham How's marvelous hymn "For All the Saints" captures something of the inspiration provided by those who, as the Apostle Paul put it, "have fought the good fight, . . . have finished the race, . . . have kept the faith" (2 Timothy 3:7):

> O blest communion, fellowship divine!
> We feebly struggle, they in glory shine;
> Yet all are one in Thee, for all are Thine.
> Alleluia! Alleluia![5]

Being faithful to the call of discipleship to Jesus Christ, no matter how hard, persevering even when one's own strength wanes, never giving up even when the cause seems beyond hope—that's both the joy and the challenge of a life of discipleship. And furthermore, in the midst of all that, we are called to urge each other on. We are better able to do that when we recall the faith and faithfulness of those on whose shoulders we stand. We are reminded not only of their faithfulness, but, more important, we are reminded of the faithfulness of the God who led them, and who leads us, through their own wilderness to the Promised Land.

Baseball is only a game. But it's a game that's played to the end with hope, determination, joy, and goodwill. We can't play it well if we are looking into the stands. But we can be inspired to try harder if we remember the labor and

5. "For All the Saints," hymn #526 in *The Presbyterian Hymnal* (Louisville: Westminster John Knox, 1990).

the interest of all those in that cloud of witnesses who are cheering us on. Just as Hall of Fame baseball players understand the game intimately and enjoy helping younger players learn, so some of those witnesses cheering us on are mentioned in the faith Hall of Fame from Hebrews 11. Indeed all the cheering fans in the stands, so to speak, have taken their places with Christ himself.

9

Home

A. Bartlett Giamatti was commissioner of baseball from April 1, 1989, until his death at the age of fifty-one years on September 1, 1989—five months. He came to the office from academia. He was a Renaissance scholar and had spent most of his academic career at Yale University, from 1978 to 1986 as its president. In 1986 he became president of the National League and served in that capacity until becoming commissioner in 1989.

Ever the Boston Red Sox fan, Giamatti had a passion for the game of baseball. Attributed to him are several memorable quotations: "There's nothing bad that accrues from baseball"; "No one man is superior to the game"; and "On matters of race, on matters of decency, baseball should lead the way." Giamatti was also the commissioner who decided that Pete Rose should be banned from baseball because he gambled on games while a player and a manager. This decree has had the effect of eliminating Rose, at least so far, from ever being considered for induction into the Hall of Fame.

In an essay titled "Baseball as Narrative," Giamatti reflects on the game and at one point considers the naming of each of the four stations on the infield. How each of the first three stations came to be called a "base" is not altogether clear. Equally unclear, and perhaps a bit more mysterious, is why the pentagram where the batter starts and where he hopes to return is not called "fourth base" but "home." Giamatti writes:

> *Home* is an English word virtually impossible to translate into other tongues. No translation catches the associations, the mixture of memory and longing, the sense of security and autonomy and accessibility, the aroma of inclusiveness, of freedom from wariness, that cling to the word *home* and are absent from *house* or even *my house. Home* is a concept, not a place; it is a state of mind where self-definition starts; it is origins—the mix of time and place and smell and weather wherein one first realizes one is an original, perhaps *like* others, especially those one loves, but discrete, distinct, not to be copied. Home is where one first learned to be separate and it remains in the mind as the place where reunion, if it ever were to occur, would happen.[1]

Giamatti continues this meditation on the infield in baseball by considering it a journey, not unlike Homer's Odysseus who ventures from home, leaving wife Penelope, and engaging in all kinds of dangers and temptations before, eventually, returning home. Giamatti also looks at the

1. "Baseball as Narrative" in Giamatti's *Take Time for Paradise: Americans and Their Games* (New York: Summit, 1989), 91–92.

development of America in terms of a search for stability, prosperity, safety—in short, home. He then applies the metaphor to baseball:

> As the heroes of romance beginning with Odysseus know, the route is full of turnings, wanderings, danger. To attempt to go home is to go the long way around, to stray and separate in the hope of finding completeness in reunion, freedom in reintegration with those left behind. In baseball, the journey begins at home, negotiates the twists and turns at first, and often founders far out at the edges of the ordered world at rocky second—the farthest point from home.
>
> Whoever remains out there is said to "die" on base. Home is finally beyond reach in a hostile world full of quirks and tricks and hostile folk. There are no dragons in baseball, only shortstops, but they can emerge from nowhere to cut one down. And when it is given one to round third, a long journey seemingly over, the end in sight, then the hunger for home, the drive to rejoin one's earlier self and one's fellows, is a pressing, growing, screaming in the blood. Often the effort fails, the hunger is unsatisfied as the catcher bars fulfillment, as the umpire-father is too strong in his denial, as the impossibility of going home again is reenacted in what is often baseball's most violent physical confrontation, swift, savage, down in the dirt, nothing availing.[2]

Giamatti maintains that while the journey is made by the players on the field, the story—the narrative—is told

2. Ibid.,93.

by the fans: "If baseball is a narrative, an epic of exile and return, a vast, communal poem about separation, loss, and the hope for reunion—if baseball is a Romance Epic—it is finally told by the audience. It is the Romance Epic of homecoming America sings to itself."[3]

Perhaps Giamatti makes too much of baseball as a "Romance Epic," comparing it to such classics as Homer's *Odyssey*. But perhaps not. Or at least it may not be too much to say that the game lends itself to broader metaphorical themes, even of biblical and theological proportions.

There are few more exciting plays than to see a player try to steal home. Jackie Robinson stole home nineteen times in his ten year career. One was in the opening game of the 1955 World Series against the New York Yankees and catcher Yogi Berra. The Dodgers won that series. Interestingly, Robinson's daughter, Sharon, titled her account of growing up in that family *Stealing Home*.[4]

For the prodigal son, home is not so much the place he has left and to which he returns as it is the realization ("when he came to himself") that he has been foolish, particularly in his family relationships, and even more specifically in that with his father. He rediscovers acceptance and love "at home."

In contrast, the older son, who never left his family's farm, continues to live "in the far country" and has not yet come to himself. Indeed, even when his father comes to him (the father taking the initiative, just as he had done so in running to greet the younger son), the older son refuses

3. Ibid., 95.

4. Sharon Robinson, *Stealing Home: An Intimate Family Portrait by the Daughter of Jackie Robinson* (New York: HarperCollins, 1996).

to allow himself to participate in the joy of his brother's homecoming. He won't allow himself to see anyone's interest other than his own.

Henri Nouwen's commentary on Rembrandt's depiction of "The Return of the Prodigal" is helpful here. He observes that "while the young man in the story seemingly left his home and lost everything, one possession remained. He was still a *member* of his family. He *belonged* to those people and to that homestead. As he moved through the pain of his disillusionment with life and himself to the awareness that there was something that could never be lost, he began his actual return."[5]

In our baptism we discover that we belong to God. God has claimed us as God's own, and has called us to be God's people. The prodigal's "coming to himself" had not only to do with his own rashness and foolishness, but also with the realization that he *belonged*—to his father, to his brother, to his family, to the entire household.

Karl Barth put it this way: "Only the son who is already recalling his father's house knows that he is a lost son. We know that we are God's enemies first and solely from the fact that God has actually established that intercourse with us. But precisely on the assumption of the factuality of this event we can regard this event itself only as miraculous."[6] Elsewhere, Barth elaborates on the place of Jesus Christ in this parable and reiterates the notion of the son's memory of membership in his family as being home: "In the parable,

5. Henri J. M. Nouwen, *Home Tonight: Further Reflections on the Parable of the Prodigal Son* (New York: Doubleday, 2009), 23.

6. Karl Barth, *Church Dogmatics* I/1 (Edinburgh: T. & T. Clark, 1975), 407.

then, Jesus is 'the running out of the father to meet his son.' Jesus is 'hidden in the kiss which the father gives his son.' Jesus is the power of the son's recollection of his father and home, and his father's fatherliness and readiness to forgive."[7]

The closing verse to Isaac Watts's adaptation of Psalm 23 in the hymn "My Shepherd Will Supply My Need" captures the twofold theme of joy and home.

> The sure provisions of my God
> Attend me all my days;
> O may Your House be my abode,
> And all my work be praise.
> There would I find a settled rest,
> While others go and come;
> No more a stranger, or a guest,
> But like a child at home.[8]

The understanding of home as baptism and forgiveness and relationship with God and others is extended to the sacrament of the Lord's Supper. The 1984 movie *Places in the Heart* depicts the survival of Edna Spalding (played by Sally Fields) and her two children on a farm in Texas after her husband has been shot and killed by an inebriated African American youngster. The setting is Waxahachie, Texas, in the 1930s. The story is about survival on a farm in the Depression, it's about race, it's about marriage, it's about faith, courage, and endurance.

One of the most striking scenes occurs at the end of the movie when Edna and her children go to church. It

7. Barth, *Church Dogmatics* IV/2 (Edinburgh: T. & T. Clark, 1975), 22.

8. "My Shepherd Will Supply My Need," hymn #172 in *The Presbyterian Hymnal* (Louisville: Westminster John Knox, 1990).

happens to be Communion Sunday. When they enter the church building, there are only a few scattered worshipers in the sanctuary. But then, as the bread and the wine are being distributed and passed along to persons in the pews, we begin to see a sanctuary that is full—full of persons who had been estranged from one another in the course of the story or persons who had even died. Edna's husband is there as is the young man who shot him and was eventually hung.

It's a powerful scene because in it everything that had happened to cause division or violence or even death no longer seemed to matter. Everyone was together around the table, sharing the bread and the cup. Everyone was home.

The kingdom of God is home, and that is where Jesus Christ is confessed as Lord. The kingdom of God is whenever and wherever we come to ourselves, acknowledge our own foolishness and sinfulness, and return to the one who created and loved us from the very beginning, and whose love is relentless. In doing so, we discover that this God has not only been waiting for us to return but, in seeing us, rushes out to welcome us home. Our joy in being home is superseded only by the joy of this God, who orders that a feast be prepared to celebrate the return of this one who was lost and is now found.

It's a similar kind of joy that baseball invites. The joy is in the game itself, not in how well or how poorly one plays (although that does make a difference to us, personally), not even in who wins or who loses (although that too makes a difference to us). Those who play, those who umpire, those who announce, those who watch the game are part of the game and, to one degree or another, participate in it. They all belong to the game. They are all at the table.

10

Extra Innings

THE collection of essays titled *The Faith of Fifty Million: Baseball, Religion, and American Culture*, edited by Christopher H. Evans and William R. Herzog II, was the first volume that, for me, took seriously the possible relationship between baseball and theology. In reading those essays I was led to further reflection on that relationship and, eventually, found the gumption to attempt this project.

Baseball is only a game. It would be too much to make it out to be more than it is. And yet, even like Jesus's parables, it contains something of a grain of truth when seen as an example of kingdom life. Whether it's such characteristics as human failure and freedom or joy or hope or community, the game of baseball exhibits qualities that at least in part resemble similar qualities in the kingdom of God.

Not only is baseball limited in its usefulness as metaphor for the kingdom, but the game itself is flawed as an example of the kingdom. While it led the nation in the drive towards eventual integration of the races, baseball was for the longest time a segregated sport. There were many great baseball players in the Negro leagues who never had the opportunity to play in the major leagues. Some might argue that, at times, the Negro league teams were every bit as good as the white major league teams, but, except for records from some exhibition games, we'll never really know how good either league would have been against the other.

Baseball, like all other professional sports, is a business and is often viewed more as a business than as a sport. Even though Curt Flood and Andy Messerschmidt led the way for players' union, free agency, and greater participation by the players in contract negotiation, the game is still a game and requires great skill to be played well.

Christopher Evans points out that, as grand as baseball is as a game, in some respects it reflects this country's tendency towards civil religion. More often, civil religion takes the form of national pride and patriotism (for example, the nineteenth-century notion of manifest destiny that persists in many circles today). Evans quotes Albert Spalding, one of the early promoters of baseball in this country: "I claim that Base Ball owes its prestige as our National Game to the fact that as no other form of sport it is the exponent of American Courage, Confidence, Combativeness; American Dash, Discipline, Determination; American Energy, Eagerness, Enthusiasm; American Pluck, Persistency, Performance; American Spirit; Sagacity, Success; American Vim, Vigor, Virility."[1]

1. Quoted in Evans's essay, "Baseball as Civil Religion: The Genesis of an American Creation Story," in Evans and Herzog, *The Faith of Fifty Million: Baseball, Religion, and American Culture* (Louisville: Westminster John Knox, 2002), 27.

Evans, a church historian, goes on to observe: "As turn-of-the century politicians believed in America's manifest destiny and as American Protestant leaders believed in 'Christianizing' the masses, so baseball symbolized an American faith that the world could be subjugated by the superior values of the United States. Baseball symbolized not only American uniqueness, but in its own way reinforced a message that God was on our side."[2]

A kind of mythology grew up around baseball as the game became increasingly popular. Rugged individualism became a part of that myth. Indeed, this part of the myth came to exclude women and African Americans, as Evans points out. Nevertheless, given the size of athletic stadiums in general and the size of the salaries of baseball players in particular, one could argue that the business of sports in America has become a religious enterprise.

In another essay, "The Kingdom of Baseball in America: The Chronicle of an American Theology," Evans notes that the ascendancy of baseball into "America's pastime" coincided with the Progressive Era when many Protestant leaders preached a gospel in which God's kingdom of social justice could be ushered in through conscientious, well-motivated laborers. According to Evans, many of these leaders saw baseball as one vehicle that could contribute to this kingdom-building effort. He identifies three themes in the rhetoric of "liberal-Protestant, Progressive-Era reformers that point to the origin of the kingdom of baseball in America": (1) "a strong vision of social progress where social reform initiatives were viewed as movements closer to the kingdom of God"; (2) the belief that baseball "embodied the virtues of

2. Ibid., 30–31.

Christian recreation"; and (3) the notion that "baseball embodied . . . the chief cornerstone of the kingdom of God in America—a faith in Christian democracy."[3]

While it may seem that Evans gives baseball too much attention, at least as far as seeing it as a participant in the life of the late nineteenth- and early twentieth-century Protestant church and much of its theology, nevertheless it does seem to be true that baseball can be seen as an active participant in a culture, the values of which were useful to and consistent with many values advocated by the church. Sometimes those values coincided with those of the church's theology, and sometimes they, like culture, resisted the values of the kingdom.

Where Evans is, in fact, very helpful is in pointing out the role of failure and grace in baseball and in the Christian faith. And it is from that point of departure that it is legitimate to compare various characteristics of the game of baseball with the points of some of Jesus's parables. As Evans and Herzog observe in the conclusion of their volume, "Baseball historically has served not as a passage to the promised land, but as a way to see grace through the unexpected—when sinners become saints and saints become sinners."[4]

May we all discover the joy of that grace.

3. Evans, "The Kingdom of Baseball in America: The Chronicle of an American Theology" ibid., 37, 39, 40. Representatives of this Social Gospel theology include Josiah Strong, Shailer Mathews, Washington Gladden, and Walter Rauschenbusch. Interestingly, the Christian athlete, or the notion of Christian recreation, was regularly promoted by popular evangelists such as former baseball player Billy Sunday, one who would not normally be counted as a Social Gospeler.

4. Evans and Herzog, "Conclusion," in ibid., 219–20.